BUILDING CONFIDENCE IN LITERACY

Jenny Thomas, Diane White
and Kathryn Ryan

Building Confidence in Literacy
1st Edition
Jenny Thomas
Diane White
Kathryn Ryan

Cover designer: Cheryl Smith, Macarn Design
Text designer: Cheryl Smith, Macarn Design

Any URLs contained in this publication were checked for currency during the production process. Note, however, that the publisher cannot vouch for the ongoing currency of URLs.

Acknowledgements
The authors and publisher wish to thank the following people and organisations for permission to use the resources in this textbook.

Page 8: *Start Smart, Hunt Better* courtesy of NZ Hunter Magazine and the NZ Game Animal Council. Page 11: *City Mission opens catering business* by Frances Chin courtesy of Stuff. Page 14: *Illustrated History of the South Pacific* by Marcia Stenson. Copyright © Marcia Stenson, 2006. First published by Random House New Zealand. This extract used by arrangement with Penguin Random House New Zealand Ltd. Page 16: *Critters of Aotearoa: 50 Bizarre But Lovable Members of Our Wildlife Community* by Nicola Toki and Lily Duval. Text Copyright © Nicola Toki, 2023. Illustrations Copyright © Lily Duval, 2023. First published by Puffin, an imprint of Penguin Random House New Zealand Ltd. This extract used by arrangement with Penguin Random House New Zealand Ltd. Page 18: *Celebrating all things heroic* courtesy of Regional News and the Porirua City Council. Page 20: *Looking at droppings* and images courtesy of NZ Hunter. Page 24: *To Sign is to be Seen* courtesy of Civil Defence. Page 26: *Thinking Big – Pōtiki Poi* by Joanna Cho and image courtesy of Ministry of Education. Page 28: *Do BLUNT umbrellas flip inside out?* courtesy of BLUNT Umbrellas NZ. Page 30: *Beyond Circular Fashion* courtesy of Zero Waste Europe, 2023. Page 34: *Zebras of the fish world use their stripes to dazzle predators* by Imma Perfetto, https://cosmosmagazine.com/© CSIRO Publishing. Reproduced with permission. Page 36: *The story behind the popular New Zealand fashion label YOUKNOW* by Fiona Connor courtesy of TVNZ. Page 38: *Discussing scam safety with your kids* courtesy of the New Zealand Herald. Page 40: *Diabetes: what you need to know and Liam's story* courtesy of Diabetes New Zealand. Page 44: *Far North author weaves Māori survival methods into kids' book* courtesy of the Northern Advocate and the New Zealand Herald. Page 45: extract from *Cuz* by Liz van der Laarse courtesy of One Tree House Ltd. No part of this work may be further reproduced without prior written permission from the copyright holder.

All other images and line drawings courtesy of Shutterstock.

For product information and technology assistance,
in Australia call **1300 790 853;**
in New Zealand call **0800 449 725**

For permission to use material from this text or product, please email **aust.permissions@cengage.com**

National Library of New Zealand Cataloguing-in-Publication Data
A catalogue record for this book is available from the National Library of New Zealand.

978 0 17 049928 6

Cengage Learning Australia
Level 5, 80 Dorcas Street
Southbank VIC 3006, Australia

Printed in China by 1010 Printing International Limited.
1 2 3 4 5 6 7 30 29 28 27 26

Please note: The way questions are written in the assessments may change from time to time. Therefore, in this workbook, the questions have been written in different ways quite deliberately. Students will benefit from the flexibility this will encourage.

CONTENTS

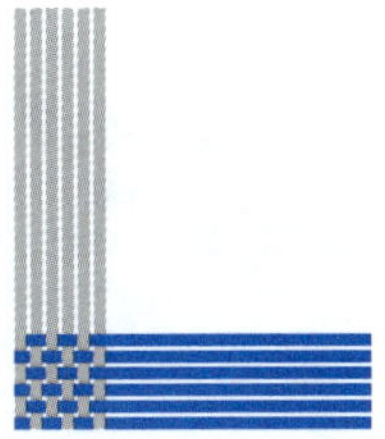

Let's get reading

Kia pānui tātou

This workbook will give you the opportunity to practise reading with purpose and **expressing your understanding** of what you read as you get ready to achieve NCEA Literacy.

In the Literacy Reading assessment, you will be directed to read several passages or texts. There will be a variety of texts, including:

- extracts from non-fiction texts
- advertisements
- posters
- extracts from novels or short stories
- web pages
- magazine articles
- blog pages
- etc.

This workbook will help you to understand what the assessment requires by showing you the sort of texts that the assessment uses, the types of question you may be asked and how to answer multi-choice questions confidently.

It will encourage you to check:

- Have you read the text completely?
- Have you understood the question?
- Have you read any more difficult sections of the text twice?
- Have you read all the possible answers?
- Have you chosen the best answer?

This workbook will build your confidence. It will encourage you to read with purpose. It will show you how to answer close reading questions with confidence.

Let's get started ...

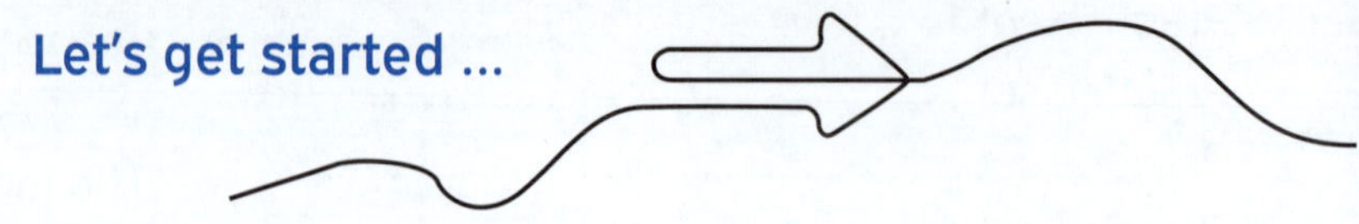

 ISBN: 9780170499286

How to read a text

To read and understand a text successfully in an assessment, it can help to follow a process. This is a good one:

1 **Read the title.**
What does it tell you about the text?

2 **Take a look at the whole text.** (Skim reading)
Does it have a specific layout like newspaper columns? Could it be online? Are there any pictures with captions, graphics, hyperlinks? Are there any subheadings, bullet points?

3 **Read the entire text.**
Read all of the text before trying to answer any of the questions.

4 Read the text **again**.
If there are words you're not sure of, read around them to try to work out the meaning.

5 Try to **answer these questions** for yourself:

- **Who** has written the text or what is the **source** of the text?
  - Is it a trustworthy text?
- **Why** has the text been written?
  - What is its purpose? For whom is it written?
- **Where** would the text be published?
  - This could be important for reaching its audience.
- **What** are the key ideas?
  - Is there a single idea or several?
  - Are there key words that link to this idea?
- **How** has the text communicated these ideas?
  - Effective words chosen, striking images, repetition, etc.

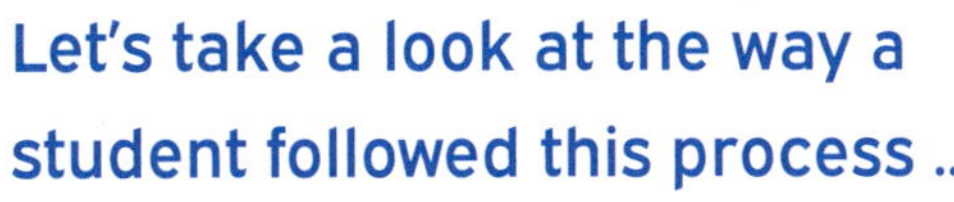

Let's take a look at the way a student followed this process ...

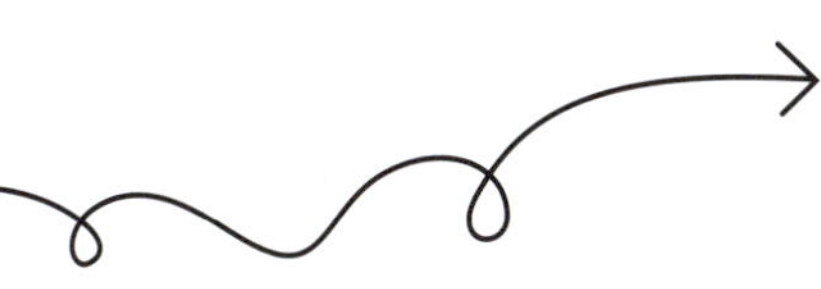

ISBN: 9780170499286

Have a go ...

Look at the student annotations on the text below and see how following this process can help you to think about an entire text before answering any of the questions.

Title says it is about a sweet dessert. Uses alliteration.

WHO? Source: a named cookbook. Seems trustworthy. Is for people who want to bake.

WHERE? In a book of recipes.

Picture to show what pavlova should look like.

WHY? To show how to make a pavlova.

WHAT? How to make a great pavlova. List of ingredients and how to combine them to make the dessert.

HOW? Quantities given. Process is in steps. Advice on what to do. Information about presentation.

Recipe with ingredient list and steps for method.

Pavlova Perfection

From the cook book *Delicious Desserts*

PREPARATION 20 MINS
BAKE 1.5 HRS
SERVINGS 12

- 6 egg whites
- 2 cups caster sugar
- 1 tsp vanilla essence
- 1 tsp white vinegar
- 2 tsp cornflour
- 300 ml whipped cream
- fruit to decorate

METHOD

1. Preheat oven to 110°C bake.
2. Line baking tray with baking paper.
3. In a large glass bowl, beat egg whites until soft peaks form.
4. Add caster sugar a little at a time and continue beating for 10 minutes until glossy.
5. Beat in vanilla, vinegar and cornflour.
6. Spoon mixture onto tray in a dinner plate size mound.
7. Bake for 1.5 hours until dry and crisp and lifts off paper.
8. Turn off oven. Leave pavlova in oven for an hour.
9. Cool on wire rack.

To serve: Top with whipped cream and fruit.

Now try answering the questions on this text. The annotations will help.

ISBN: 9780170499286

Select (✓) the correct answer to the multiple-choice questions below.

1 Where was this text published?

- (A) In a picture book.
- (B) On the internet.
- (C) In a book of recipes.
- (D) In a text called Pavlova Perfection.

2 Why is a picture included in this text?

- (A) To show what a dessert looks like.
- (B) To show the reader what their own pavlova could look like.
- (C) To show the ingredients in a pavlova.
- (D) To attract attention.

3 How is the information made easy to follow?

- (A) It is in a clear font.
- (B) It is written with numbers.
- (C) It is given in a list of ingredients and steps for mixing the pavlova.
- (D) It is written with times and temperatures.

4 How long will the pavlova be inside the oven?

- (A) Two and a half hours in total.
- (B) An hour and fifty minutes.
- (C) 1.5 hours.
- (D) One and a half hours.

5 Which word best replaces the word 'Method' in this text?

- (A) Approach
- (B) Technique
- (C) Recipe
- (D) Instructions

Here is a quick reference to a plan of action, a reading strategy, for you to use. Use it for every text you are asked about.

Who has written the text or what is the **source** of the text?
Why has the text been written?
Where would the text be published?
What are the key ideas?
How has the text communicated these ideas?

Read on to discover more about reading strategies.

Let's take a closer look

Here you will be able to see the way one student used the quick reference list to think about the answers to the questions carefully.

Start Smart, Hunt Better

Read the text below from the *NZ Hunter Magazine* and answer the questions that follow.

Start Smart, Hunt Better: Free Courses from NZ Game Animal Council

Better Hunting is a free online training platform built by the NZ Game Animal Council to help hunters improve their skills and knowledge, while helping them understand their obligations and responsibilities as hunters and firearms users.

The courses and resources are intended to provide a pathway and support hunters who go on to do practical training, such as the NZDA HUNTS courses.

The content is designed by New Zealand hunters, for New Zealand hunters. You can do the courses on your phone and even download them for offline viewing using the app.

For new, inexperienced and casual hunters, the two main courses, Hunting Essentials and Firearm Essentials, cover foundational hunting and outdoor skills. There's also an Introduction to Pig Hunting course.

More experienced hunters will still find useful information throughout many of the modules, in maps, forecasts, hunting and ballot calendars, intentions form or games. Each module has a short quiz and there are assessments you can do to ensure your knowledge is up to date.

Visit betterhunting.nz to check it out. If you enjoy using it, please share it around.

BETTERHUNTING.NZ

STOP AND THINK

WHO wrote the text/the source of the text? *NZ Game Animal Council; nationwide council = trust*

WHY was the text written? *Informative and persuasive piece – informs us of an app designed to educate hunters. Call to action – download the free app and complete the courses.*

WHERE was the text published? NZ Hunter Magazine. *Magazines are usually considered reliable.*

WHAT are the key ideas? *Promoting local online resource for NZ hunters to improve skills.*

HOW has the text communicated these ideas? *Is from official organisation. By giving examples of interesting ways to do the work. Repeats 'New Zealand' and 'NZ' a lot. Advises action: do, download, etc.*

ISBN: 9780170499286

A student who answered the questions on this text has told us how they used their close reading skills to select the best answer. Check their answer and then read about how they arrived at the selection they made.

1 Which course is aimed at new and inexperienced hunters?

- (A) Hunting Essentials and Firearm Essentials
- (B) Introduction to Pig Hunting
- (C) How to Read a Map
- (D) Practical Training

How do I know? I **checked** the article looking for capital letters mid-sentence. Found 'Hunting Essentials and Firearm Essentials', **stopped and read** the full sentence. It states that 'For new, inexperienced and casual hunters, the two main courses, Hunting Essentials and Firearm Essentials, cover foundational hunting and outdoor skills.'

2 What feature helps users check they've understood the content of each module?

- (A) Links to expert hunting blogs.
- (B) Live chat with certified trainers.
- (C) A short quiz and assessments.
- (D) Community discussion boards.

How do I know? I **scanned** the article looking for the **keyword 'module'**. When I found it in the text, I **reread** the sentence that included the word and the one before it. It told me that there are short quizzes and assessments 'to ensure your knowledge is up to date'. This links most clearly to the question of checking understanding.

3 Select the best word to replace 'obligations' in the text below:

*'... help hunters improve their skills and knowledge, while helping them understand their **obligations** and responsibilities as hunters and firearms users.'*

- (A) duties
- (B) debts
- (C) worries
- (D) chores

How do I know? I tried **each word in the sentence**, reading it in my head to see if it made sense in terms of what I understand the sentence to mean, and what I know or think each of the alternative words mean. The one most similar to responsibilities is duties and this is also the one that makes the most sense in the sentence.

4 Which of the following is most relevant when judging whether this site is a reliable source?

- (A) The inclusion of colourful images and video clips.
- (B) That it was created by the NZ Game Animal Council.
- (C) The ability to share the link with friends.
- (D) That it is free.

How do I know? I read the answer options carefully in terms of **reliability**. D, A and C do not mean something is reliable. However, NZ stands for New Zealand, so it is the New Zealand Game Animal Council. This means that a council that is responsible for all of New Zealand built this training platform, which means it is a reliable source.

Now, try these questions yourself.

5 What is the most likely reason that '*designed by New Zealand hunters, for New Zealand hunters*' is included?

- (A) To highlight that the content has been tested by government officials.
- (B) To warn that international users may not find it relevant.
- (C) To indicate that the content has been endorsed by all hunting organisations.
- (D) To build trust by showing it's made by people with local experience.

How do I know?

6 What is the main reason NZ Game Animal Council asked for their website to be shared around?

- (A) To make money.
- (B) To promote safe hunting practices.
- (C) To advertise their business.
- (D) To gain more followers on social media.

How do I know?

7 This article is called Start Smart, Hunt Better. What does this mean?

- (A) Clever people make good hunters.
- (B) If you learn skills first you will be a more successful hunter.
- (C) You will be a better hunter if you dress smartly.
- (D) Do courses in hunting when you know what you need.

How do I know?

8 Why should a hunter do the quizzes and assessments on the website?

- (A) Because they are fun to do.
- (B) Because the questions are easy.
- (C) Because they help to check if the hunter's knowledge is up to date.
- (D) Because they are short and quick to answer.

How do I know?

Let's practise more close reading ...

 ISBN: 9780170499286

Let's read together

In the next couple of texts, we've offered you some help with answering the questions. You'll find annotations in the passages and a few helpful clues beside the questions to guide your thinking. Use this as a chance to practise your skills and build your confidence in close reading.

TEXT 1

Read the text below from a newspaper article in *The Post* and answer the questions that follow.

Where: Wellington newspaper or their website.

Who: Author and source.

A key idea of the text.

Why: To inform.

How: Used repetition: needy, proceeds.

How: Used examples.

A key idea of the text.

City Mission opens catering business

by Frances Chin

Wellington City Mission has launched a catering service, with all the proceeds going towards feeding the capital's needy.

Called Craig & Gail's Community Conscious Catering, the service offers a number of high-quality nibbles – including sandwiches, muffins, doughnuts, scones, slices, and biscuits – to be ordered in bulk through their website.

Prices range from $65 for a cheese scone platter, to $196 for a box of 16 filled baguettes – and all the proceeds will go towards the Wellington City Mission, Wellington City Missioner Murray Edridge says.

Operating out of Whakamaru, Wellington City Mission's Shelter facility in Mt Cook, the food is prepared there before being transported by a team of volunteers to the recipients.

Additionally, any food left over could be reclaimed by the City Mission and spread out among the needy if the customer desired, Edridge said.

"People over-cater because people are generous by nature. So what we've said in this model is, if you have food left over, we will come and pick it up and we'll redistribute it," he said.

"People get great quality catering at market rates, but then the proceeds will go to supporting the City Mission."

Whakamaru opened in October, after Wellington City Mission fundraised $4.5 million to go towards the construction of the community hub.

A key idea of the text.

How: Used quotations.

STOP AND THINK

WHO wrote the text/the source of the text?
WHY was the text written?
WHERE was the text published?
WHAT are the key ideas?
HOW has the text communicated these ideas?

Work your way through this checklist, annotating the passage as you go. It is helpful to make sure that you understand the text before you start the questions.

Select (✓) the correct answer to the multiple-choice questions below.

1 What is Wellington City Mission?

- (A) A catering business.
- (B) A place where people can order food.
- (C) An organisation that looks after people in need in Wellington City.
- (D) A business in Wellington City with a mission.

The answer for this question may not be right there in front of you. You will have to look for some clues and make some links. Another way to look at this is by reading the whole passage, you can work out which of the answers are incorrect.

2 Why is the title of this piece used?

- (A) It says the item is about Wellington City Mission.
- (B) It makes the reader wonder how a City Mission charity and a catering business work together.
- (C) It asks the reader a question.
- (D) It shows how anyone can be a caterer.

Go back and look at the title. Notice that only one answer gives both sides.

3 How does this business avoid one expense?

The answer for this is right there in the passage. A clue is the word 'expense'.

- (A) They make the food at the Whakamaru Shelter.
- (B) If too much food is made, they go and collect it.
- (C) A team of volunteers delivers the food so those workers do not get paid.
- (D) They redistribute leftover food.

4 Who are the *recipients* of the platters of food?

- (A) The needy.
- (B) People in the shelter.
- (C) Customers who order the high-quality nibbles.
- (D) Whakamaru residents.

Find the word 'recipients' in the passage and read around it. Then go back and look at the options.

5 What do the words in bold mean?

*'... feeding the **capital's needy**.'*

We hope you know which city is the capital of New Zealand!

- (A) People who need help in Wellington.
- (B) People who need help in Auckland.
- (C) People who need help in a city.
- (D) People who need help in a big city.

ISBN: 9780170499286

6 How much did Wellington City Mission contribute to establishing Whakamaru?

(A) 4.5
(B) $4.5
(C) $4.5 million
(D) $45 million

The answer is right there in the text. Be careful to pick the correct option. It is easy to make a silly mistake.

7 What does Murray Edridge say makes this a great idea for two groups of people?

(A) The people who buy the food get great nibbles and over-cater.
(B) The people who need food can have any leftover nibbles from the caterer.
(C) The caterers support the needy by selling too much food.
(D) People can help the City Mission but also get great food for their events.

Look for the name 'Edridge' and read what he says. Then read the options to pick the one that is the best answer.

8 *Craig & Gail's Community Conscious Catering*. What do you notice about the way this company name sounds?

(A) It is run by Craig and Gail and sounds friendly.
(B) Craig and Gail want to help their community.
(C) Most words begin with the letter c so they sound the same at the beginning (alliteration).
(D) Catering is a word meaning food.

Look for the answer relating to sound.

9 What does 'People get great quality catering at market rates ...' mean?

(A) The food is excellent.
(B) The food is expensive.
(C) The food is rated highly.
(D) The food costs about the same as other similar good quality food.

Look for the answer that mentions quality **and** cost.

10 Where would someone read this article?

(A) In a newspaper.
(B) In Wellington.
(C) In *The Post* newspaper or on its website.
(D) On the internet.

This question is asking you to think about where you would most likely find this article. Look for clues in the information around the text that show where it comes from, then decide which option is the best answer. Don't forget that some options might seem similar, but one of them will always be more correct.

Read the extract below from the book *Illustrated History of the South Pacific* and answer the questions that follow.

Niue

by Marcia Stenson

Geographic facts

- With a land area of 259 km^2, Niue is the world's smallest self-governing state.
- It is an isolated rocky island 2200 km north-east of New Zealand.
- Because it sits up out of the ocean like a cake on a plate it is often called 'The Rock'.
- The capital is Alofi.

First settlers

Between 1500 and 1000 years ago, sea travellers arrived from Tonga and Samoa. We know this from the Tongan and Samoan words in the Niuean language. **There were probably several waves of migration.** They named their new home after the coconut they saw growing there: Niue comes from a phrase which means 'Behold the coconut!'

The new settlers found a single uplifted coral island surrounded by rugged cliffs and a fringing reef. Most of the coastline rises 20 to 30 metres straight up out of the sea. Small canoes could be carried down the cliffs to fish in open sea. Fresh water **was, and still is**, scarce. The soil is fertile but thin. Nearly half of Niue is outcrops of hard reef rock. Growing crops **was, and still is**, difficult. Taro **was, and still is**, the main food crop. Some volcanic stone was imported for adzes, but most tools were made from coral and clam shell.

Being a chief was not passed on from father to son. Instead, the elders of each extended family had speaking rights when decisions came up. Specialists, like the priest, had to do their own fishing and growing food. Life was hard on Niue and there was no spare food. There was bitter fighting between the tribes.

Work your way through this checklist, annotating the passage as you go. It is helpful to make sure that you understand the text before you start the questions.

STOP AND THINK

WHO wrote the text/the source of the text?
WHY was the text written?
WHERE was the text published?
WHAT are the key ideas?
HOW has the text communicated these ideas?

 ISBN: 9780170499286

Select (✓) the correct answer to the multiple-choice questions below.

1 Where does the name of the South Pacific island Niue come from?

- Ⓐ From a Tongan word for coconut.
- Ⓑ From a Samoan word meaning coconut.
- Ⓒ From a phrase meaning 'behold the coconut'.
- Ⓓ From sea travellers.

> Questions like this are designed to check that you have read all of the passage. The answer is easily found in the text. Scan for mentions of Niue and read around each mention.

2 What does this sentence mean?

'There were probably several waves of migration.'

- Ⓐ There might have been groups of new arrivals at different times.
- Ⓑ There were definitely groups of new arrivals at different times.
- Ⓒ New arrivals came by sea.
- Ⓓ The waves brought new people to Niue.

> When you are given a sentence, it is best to go back to the text and reread the sentence before and after it. Notice that the sentence uses the key word **probably**. How many of the answers use a similar word/phrase?

3 In paragraph 2, the writer repeats the words 'was, and still is'. Why?

- Ⓐ To emphasise to the reader that life on Niue is as difficult now as it was a thousand years go.
- Ⓑ To tell the reader about life on Niue.
- Ⓒ To remind the reader that life on Niue was difficult.
- Ⓓ To emphasise that fresh water and fertile soil are in short supply.

> When you are given a direct reference point, find that part of the passage and reread it to help you choose the correct answer.

4 Why do you think most tools were made of coral and clam shell?

- Ⓐ Coral and clam shell were good materials to use for tools.
- Ⓑ Coral and clam shell could be sharpened.
- Ⓒ Coral and clam shell were available on Niue.
- Ⓓ Coral and clam shell were not volcanic.

> Note the first four words of each of the answer options are the same. That means you need to work out only which of the ends is the 'most correct' according to the text.

5 What best sums up the main idea of the paragraph beginning '*The new settlers* ...'?

- Ⓐ Niue is a steep cliff-edged island.
- Ⓑ Niue does not have lots of sandy beaches.
- Ⓒ Niue would be a difficult place to fish from.
- Ⓓ Niue is a challenging place to live.

> If you are asked to 'sum up' some text, you are being asked to give an 'overall' idea. It is not about individual parts of the paragraph but what links all those parts.

6 The text says specialists, like priests, on Niue had to do their own fishing and growing food. What does this **suggest** about life for priests on **other** Pacific Islands?

- Ⓐ Priests on other Islands were special.
- Ⓑ Priests on other Islands grew their own food.
- Ⓒ Priests on other Islands had an easier life than those on Niue.
- Ⓓ Priests on other Islands lived in the same way as those on Niue.

> This question asks you to think beyond the text's statement. What do the words imply?

Now that you've worked through a couple of texts with our support, it's time to go it alone ...

ISBN: 9780170499286

Your turn

You are ready to find your own answers. Remember, read the text and questions carefully.

Read the information below from the book *Critters of Aotearoa* and answer the questions that follow.

CICADAS/KIHIKIHI/TĀTARAKIHI

by Nicola Toki

New Zealand is a pretty exciting place for cicadas – we have about 40 species, and all of them are *endemic* to Aotearoa. Around the world there are about 2500 species, but our 40 are found only here.

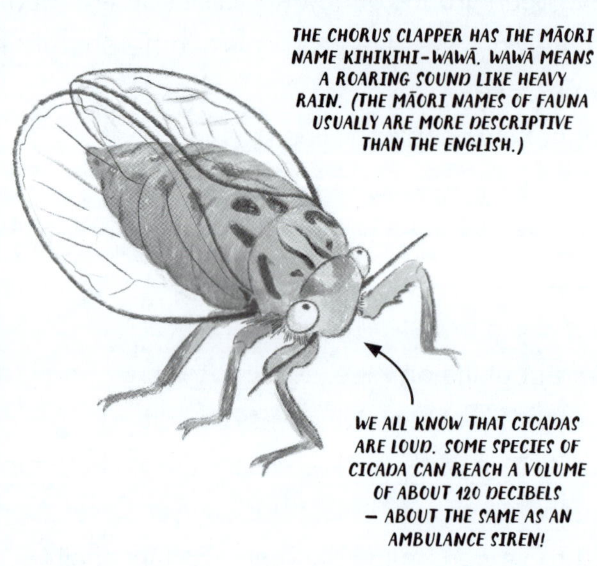

Most of the time these insects live under the soil in the nymph stage of their life cycle. After what can be several years (there's one species in America that stays underground for 17 years) they come up to the surface and make a racket to attract other cicadas so they can reproduce.

It's the males that make all the noise. Wētā, for example, make their noise by stridulating their legs, like strumming a washboard in a hillbilly band, but the cicada makes its noise through a tymbal. This 'instrument' is a membrane on the side of its abdomen. When the cicada flexes or vibrates, the tymbal pops in and out – just like when you grab a large empty soft-drink bottle and squeeze it and it does that bang-bang sound, but a cicada does it really fast – up to 600 times a second!

For early Māori, the chit-chatting of first European or English settlers was really mysterious – they couldn't understand a lot of it – so they described the chatter of the new arrivals as **te reo kihikihi**, or cicada language, because to their ears the sounds seemed really harsh.

The way to tell the difference between cicada species is their **very distinctive songs**, and that different species sing at different times of year. Clapping cicada only live in the North Island, and they start singing before Christmas. From January, you're likely to hear the delightfully named chorus clapper.

Cicadas can live in forest, rocks, scrub, tussock, grassland, riverbeds, clay banks – pretty much everywhere. A species that's part of a group known as Maoricicada lives in alpine zones – some as high as 1800 metres above sea level. Apart from habitat and sound, it's very difficult to figure them all out!

endemic: found in only one place

STOP AND THINK

WHO wrote the text/the source of the text?
WHY was the text written?
WHERE was the text published?
WHAT are the key ideas?
HOW has the text communicated these ideas?

ISBN: 9780170499286

Select (✓) the correct answer to the multiple-choice questions below.

1 How many species of cicada are found only in New Zealand?

- (A) 2500
- (B) 40
- (C) 17
- (D) 600

2 What is the cicada's noise compared with?

- (A) Strumming a washboard.
- (B) The sound of people chatting.
- (C) An empty soft-drink bottle being squeezed.
- (D) Singing at Christmas.

3 Do female cicadas make the noise?

- (A) Sometimes.
- (B) No.
- (C) Yes.
- (D) Only in alpine zones.

4 Why did Māori call the sound of early settlers' language **te reo kihikihi**?

- (A) Because they couldn't understand it.
- (B) Because they thought it sounded harsh.
- (C) Because they found it mystifying and strange.
- (D) All of these answers.

5 Where is the tymbal that makes the cicada's sound?

- (A) On its legs.
- (B) In its mouth.
- (C) On its abdomen.
- (D) On a membrane.

6 How loud can the sound of the cicada be?

- (A) Very loud.
- (B) As loud as an ambulance siren.
- (C) Like the sound of heavy rain.
- (D) A loud bang-bang sound.

7 Why is the illustration added to the description?

- (A) To show what a cicada looks like in reality.
- (B) To suggest a cicada is a pretty insect.
- (C) To make the cicada look friendly and lovable.
- (D) To show that a cicada can fly.

8 Which word is the best substitute for 'very distinctive' in this line?

> *'The way to tell the difference between cicada species is their **very distinctive** songs, ...'*

- (A) common
- (B) unique
- (C) clear
- (D) similar

ISBN: 9780170499286

Read the text below from a community newspaper and answer the questions that follow.

CELEBRATING ALL THINGS HEROIC

Heroes can be found in the most **unlikely** places, and on Sunday the 2nd March, you'll be able to find loads of them at Porirua City Council's free Te Rā o Ngā Tamariki/Children's Day event.

Celebrations of the **annual** day recognising our tamariki will run from 11am to 3pm at Ngāti Toa Domain in Paremata. The theme for the day is all things heroic – this could be everyday heroes, superheroes, or community heroes, and hopefully the event will **inspire some heroes of tomorrow**.

Visitors of all ages are encouraged to dress up as their favourite type of hero, with lots of cool prizes to be won. "Children are such an important part of our city, and as about 40 percent of Porirua's population is younger than 25, it's only fair that we use this day to put them first," Porirua mayor Anita Baker says. "Celebrating all things heroic will give tamariki the chance to meet everyday heroes from our community such as those who work hard for our emergency and health services, and our environmental heroes too."

Attendees can meet and chat with representatives from local emergency services, Whānau Āwhina Plunket, Bee Healthy Regional Dental Service, Ora Toa, Surf Lifesaving NZ, Predator Free NZ Trust and Nonstop Solutions.

There will also be loads of opportunities for tākaro **(play)** activities for all ages – from a preschool area to giant games, a colouring station, free face painting, and many, many inflatables.

Find out more at www.poriruacity.govt.nz/children'sday.

STOP AND THINK

WHO wrote the text/the source of the text?
WHY was the text written?
WHERE was the text published?
WHAT are the key ideas?
HOW has the text communicated these ideas?

 ISBN: 9780170499286

Select (✓) the correct answer to the multiple-choice questions below.

1 Which word best replaces **unlikely** in this sentence?

*'Heroes can be found in the most **unlikely** places.'*

- (A) unconvincing
- (B) unexpected
- (C) remote
- (D) strange

2 Approximately what percentage of people in Porirua are older than 25?

- (A) 40 percent
- (B) 60 percent
- (C) About half
- (D) More than half

3 What does the text want people to do before they come to the event?

- (A) Dress up.
- (B) Dress up as a hero of some sort.
- (C) Dress up as a superhero.
- (D) Dress up as their favourite hero.

4 What is the theme for this day?

- (A) Children having fun.
- (B) Being a superhero.
- (C) Meeting different types of heroes in our community.
- (D) Dressing up as a hero.

5 What does the writer mean by saying the following?

*'... hopefully the event will **inspire some heroes of tomorrow**.'*

- (A) Children might grow up to be heroes.
- (B) Children may want jobs as firefighters or dentists.
- (C) Children may feel influenced to do helpful things when they grow up.
- (D) Children will see good role models.

6 What does the word '*annual*' mean?

- (A) Once a year.
- (B) Every six months.
- (C) Every other year.
- (D) Every 10 years.

7 Why is the word '*play*' inside brackets?

*'There will also be loads of opportunities for tākaro **(play)** activities for all ages ...'*

- (A) It translates into English the Māori word tākaro.
- (B) It is to explain the meaning of the word tākaro for people who don't understand Māori.
- (C) It is not necessary if the reader understands Māori.
- (D) All of the above.

8 What has the city done to attract families to this event?

- (A) Provided games for children to play.
- (B) Made it free.
- (C) Provided games and prizes to be won.
- (D) Made it free and provided prizes and games.

Read the abridged article below from the magazine *NZ Hunter* and answer the questions that follow.

Looking at droppings

Little excites a hunter more than chancing upon fresh animal droppings – it means something is close by!

Let's see how to get the most out of your chance encounter with these treasures.

DIFFERENT STRUCTURES – CLUMPS OR PELLETS

Depending on the diet, animal droppings can be either clumped or separate pellets. Pellets are more common when an animal has a lot of fibre (think vegetation) in their diet and little else.

Pellets are easier to assess than clumps. Every pellet provides a **nugget of information**.

Let's see what a dropping can tell you.

Size of animal

The size of the dropping can suggest the size of the animal; both in the girth and the rectal cavity that passed it, and the amount of droppings deposited. If you've spent any time around small dogs you'll know it's not an exact science – at times **the smallest animals can make the biggest messes**.

Diet of animal

You may be able to see what the animal has been eating from the bits remaining in its droppings. This is more likely during the dry months, as dry vegetation is harder to digest. Seeing what the animal has been eating, if you know your hunting area well you may be able to check places with that vegetation for further signs.

When they were there

The obvious thing to assess from droppings is freshness, i.e. when the animal was there. Though the weather plays a major part in dropping decomposition, generally:

- Warm droppings are super fresh.
- Shiny and wet droppings are within a few hours.
- Dry, well-formed droppings are days old.
- Droppings that are breaking down or very desiccated are weeks or more old.

WEATHERING

A dropping weathers from the outside in, and the outside shell can weather and dry very quickly. So, if you're enthusiastic about assessments, consider breaking them apart. If the middle is still moist, it's still a reasonably fresh dropping.

STOP AND THINK

WHO wrote the text/the source of the text?
WHY was the text written?
WHERE was the text published?
WHAT are the key ideas?
HOW has the text communicated these ideas?

ISBN: 9780170499286

Select (✓) the correct answer to the multiple-choice questions below.

1 Why do hunters get excited when they find fresh droppings?

- (A) It means an animal may be nearby.
- (B) It helps them train dogs.
- (C) It keeps the forest clean.
- (D) It shows where to set up camp.

2 What type of droppings are easier to assess?

- (A) Clumps
- (B) Wet ones
- (C) Pellets
- (D) Ones from dry weather

3 Which word could best replace '***desiccated***' in this sentence?

'Droppings that are breaking down or very ***desiccated*** *are weeks or more old.'*

- (A) moist
- (B) dried out
- (C) sticky
- (D) shiny

4 What does the writer suggest by saying the following?

'... the smallest animals can make the biggest messes.'

- (A) Hunters should avoid small animals.
- (B) Size of droppings isn't always a reliable clue.
- (C) Big messes mean big animals.
- (D) All small dogs are messy.

5 What does '***weathering***' mean in this article?

- (A) The temperature around the animal.
- (B) How to check the weather.
- (C) When it rains heavily on the ground.
- (D) How droppings change over time due to the environment.

6 Why might breaking apart a dropping help a hunter?

- (A) To throw it further.
- (B) To hide it from others.
- (C) To check if it's fresh on the inside.
- (D) To mix it with soil.

7 Why does the writer use casual phrases like '***nugget of information***' *and* '***biggest messes***'?

- (A) To make the article sound scientific.
- (B) To confuse the reader with slang.
- (C) To sound humorous and relatable for the audience.
- (D) To show that droppings are not important.

8 How would this text be useful for a reader of *NZ Hunter*?

- (A) To write a report about animal anatomy.
- (B) To compare different animal species.
- (C) To learn how to make fertiliser.
- (D) To help identify signs of nearby animals when outdoors.

ISBN: 9780170499286

Read the text below, an extract from a newspaper article called *He Manu Taonga*, and answer the questions that follow.

HE MANU TAONGA

by Andrew James

Kiwi last walked the hills of Wellington a century ago, but the Capital Kiwi Project is bringing them back. Removing stoats from 23,000 hectares of farm, scrub and bush on the capital's hilly south coast to create a safe habitat has been a **mammoth undertaking** including iwi, landowners and the community.

. . .

[Eleven kiwi are welcomed onto the Waiwhētu Marae.]

. . .

I meet with about a dozen others outside a rural school and load into a 4WD van to travel off-road to the release site on Terawhiti Station, a large farm block south of Mākara.

It's rugged country; scrappy scrub hangs on steep hills beneath wind turbines. Cows graze in paddocks behind a sign that shows kiwi live here. People live here too. The project area isn't a reserve or a national park. It's farms, forestry and suburbs.

The southerly wind brings a few ice-cold raindrops. Goats and rabbits cross the roads. It might not look like much, but the **remnant bush and scrub** between the paddocks is rich with bugs, grubs and worms – kiwi kai. I quickly capture views out the window as we meander through the **twisty** roads following the car with the birds in it. I spot some of the black and orange stoat traps that make it all possible.

The sun's going down. It's cold and windy and starting to get dark, but there's still a buzz among the group as we make it to the first release site.

Kiwi rangers Jeff and Rawiri carefully take the box over a fence. Opening it a crack, Jeff peers in, working out which way the bird is facing. His hands reach in, securing her dinosaur feet and cradling the bird as he passes it to Ali Houpapa, one of the women who called us onto the marae. She names the bird and says a brief karakia, a blessing, before placing her legs carefully on the ground. The kiwi doesn't stop to look around; **as soon as she's let go, the manu is full speed ahead and vanishes into the scrub**.

manu = bird
taonga = treasure

STOP AND THINK

WHO wrote the text/the source of the text?
WHY was the text written?
WHERE was the text published?
WHAT are the key ideas?
HOW has the text communicated these ideas?

 ISBN: 9780170499286

Select (✓) the correct answer to the multiple-choice questions below.

1 This text is an extract. What does extract mean in this sense?

- (A) Part of a text being removed.
- (B) Half a text.
- (C) A short passage taken from a longer text.
- (D) A missing part of a text.

2 What does ***a 'mammoth undertaking'*** mean?

- (A) A huge task.
- (B) An easy job.
- (C) A routine project.
- (D) A tricky promise.

3 How long ago were kiwi last living on the Wellington hills? Two answers are correct.

- (A) A century ago.
- (B) A centenary ago.
- (C) A long time ago.
- (D) 100 years ago.

4 Why does the text say people taking the kiwi to their new home have to travel in a 4WD?

- (A) It's easier because the road is rough.
- (B) It is because the route is off-road.
- (C) The route is unpaved and therefore needs a special vehicle.
- (D) It's safer because the route is longer.

5 Why is the '***remnant bush and scrub***' good for kiwi?

- (A) It is a rich area.
- (B) There are rabbit and goats nearby.
- (C) It has lots of kai (food) for them like bugs, grubs and worms.
- (D) It will help to hide them.

6 Which word would best replace the word '**twisty**'?

*'... we meander through the **twisty** roads ...'*

- (A) bumpy
- (B) straight
- (C) hilly
- (D) winding

7 The writer says that even though it's cold and dark, there's still a buzz among the group. Why?

- (A) They are happy that the trip will be finished soon.
- (B) They are getting close to the place where the kiwi will be released.
- (C) They are all making a noise that sounds like bees.
- (D) They are all chatting with each other.

8 What is the writer showing about the kiwi in these words?

'... as soon as she's let go, the manu is full speed ahead and vanishes into the scrub.'

- (A) The bird disappears into the scrub.
- (B) The bird races off away from the people.
- (C) The bird is happy to be free.
- (D) All of these.

Read the poster below and answer the questions that follow.

TO SIGN IS TO BE SEEN

Everyone has the right to accessible information in an emergency. **NZ Sign Language (NZSL) interpreters help keep the Deaf community safe and informed.**

They should be considered an extension of the spokesperson. Including an interpreter means you're including the Deaf community.

Here are some tips so you can help NZSL interpreters get important messages across.

Fully framed in shot

Free of obstructions

Free of distractions

AND REMEMBER:

- At the start, ensure all in attendance (e.g. camera operators) understand what is needed.
- Plan ahead - when booking an interpreter, give them as much notice as possible.
- Help the interpreter prep - allow time to walk them through what's planned and share key talking points in advance.
- Seek the interpreter's advice to ensure they're comfortable with lighting, positioning, etc.
- Stream it online so Deaf audiences can view the whole thing.
- When filming, wait until the interpreter has finished signing before you cut away.

STOP AND THINK

WHO wrote the text/the source of the text?
WHY was the text written?
WHERE was the text published?
WHAT are the key ideas?
HOW has the text communicated these ideas?

 ISBN: 9780170499286

Select (✓) the correct answer to the multiple-choice questions below.

1 Which of the following advice is listed under the three smaller images on the poster?

- (A) Keep the camera on the speaker only.
- (B) Stream it online.
- (C) Keep the interpreter fully framed in shot.
- (D) Use large text on screen.

2 What does the poster say you should do before filming starts?

- (A) Wait to see who arrives.
- (B) Let the interpreter decide what to do.
- (C) Make sure everyone understands what is needed.
- (D) Ask the Deaf community to join late.

3 Which word or words could replace '**important**' in the text below?

*'... help NZSL interpreters get **important** messages across.'*

- (A) ordinary
- (B) entertaining
- (C) essential
- (D) day to day

4 What does the word '**accessible**' mean in this sentence?

*'Everyone has the right to **accessible** information in an emergency.'*

- (A) complicated
- (B) easy to reach or understand
- (C) expensive
- (D) short

5 What is the main role of NZSL interpreters during emergencies?

- (A) To stop background noise.
- (B) To run the livestream.
- (C) To film emergency videos.
- (D) To help keep the Deaf community safe and informed.

6 Why is it suggested that the interpreter be fully framed in the shot?

- (A) So their outfit is seen.
- (B) To follow media rules.
- (C) So the Deaf audience can clearly see the signing.
- (D) To include the camera operator.

7 Which feature of this poster makes it more trustworthy?

- (A) It includes logos of reputable agencies.
- (B) It has images.
- (C) It uses jokes to sound friendly.
- (D) It includes opinions about NZSL.

ISBN: 9780170499286

Read the extract below from an article in the *School Journal, June 2024* and answer the questions that follow.

Thinking Big – Pōtiki Poi

by Joanna Cho

When Georgia Latu was twelve years old, she wanted to attend a wānanga. But there was a problem. The wānanga was in Matatā, and she lived in Ōtepoti. Travel was expensive – how would she get there?

Then Georgia's mum had an idea. Georgia was good at making poi – she often made them as gifts for family and friends. Why not sell a few to make some pūtea? So Georgia posted on social media and waited. Within a few days, she'd sold dozens of poi and raised a thousand dollars. She was shocked by her success, but it got her thinking. Clearly there was a demand for poi. Maybe the idea had a future ... and maybe that future could involve more than just fundraising.

Four years later, Pōtiki Poi makes the biggest number of poi in the world. Georgia's business has an office and a website and provides work for around forty people. More importantly, it has a kaupapa that makes her proud. "Ever since I was a little girl, I've been drawn to everything Māori: weaving, mahi toi, tītī tōrea ... anything." Ultimately, Georgia's vision is for Pōtiki Poi to uplift her culture and her people, and that means helping to revitalise taonga like poi.

A strong identity

Georgia is Māori (Kāi Tahu, Ngāpuhi), Samoan, and Tokelauan. When she was younger, she went to kōhanga reo. Now she goes to Te Kura Kaupapa Māori o Ōtepoti. Learning about mātauranga Māori, and finding her people, has given Georgia a strong sense of identity. "When I started kura, there were only nine of us – we were a really tight-knit group. I have friends who've grown up in mainstream schools, and some have struggled to find their whānau. You need to find people on the same journey."

Georgia called on this community when Pōtiki Poi faced its biggest challenge yet – an order for the Women's Rugby World Cup in 2022. At first, two thousand poi were needed. Georgia said it would take two weeks. But the number kept rising. Georgia found herself making 27,000 poi! To fill the massive order, she sent out a tono, asking for help. "We were overwhelmed with support," she remembers. "There were people from church and from school – everyone wanted to help us grow the kaupapa."

A huge crowd used Georgia's poi at the World Cup final at Eden Park. She says she'll never forget the experience. It made her "very emotional" to see taonga Māori normalised and uplifted. "It was the first time something like that had ever happened," she says, "and we were part of it!" It was easy to spot their poi in the crowd: they had the traditional twisted cord, not cord that had been braided.

ISBN: 9780170499286

Select (✓) the correct answer to the multiple-choice questions below.

> **STOP AND THINK**
>
> **WHO** wrote the text/the source of the text?
> **WHY** was the text written?
> **WHERE** was the text published?
> **WHAT** are the key ideas?
> **HOW** has the text communicated these ideas?

1 Why does Joanna Cho end the first paragraph of her article with a question?

- (A) Because she wants to know the answer.
- (B) Because Georgia asked that question.
- (C) Because the question attracts attention.
- (D) Because the article is going to answer that question.

2 What was Georgia's mum's great idea?

- (A) She thought Georgia could make gifts for the family.
- (B) She suggested Georgia could sell her poi.
- (C) She said Georgia's poi were good quality.
- (D) She suggested selling poi to sports supporters.

3 How are Georgia's poi recognisable from other poi?

- (A) The poi have tassels.
- (B) The poi have a twisted cord.
- (C) The poi are all the same colour.
- (D) The poi have a braided cord.

4 How old was Georgia Latu when this article was written?

- (A) 14
- (B) 12
- (C) 16
- (D) 13

5 Which two words can replace the two words in bold in this sentence:

'She was ***shocked*** *by her success, but it got her* ***thinking****.'*

- (A) amazed, contemplating.
- (B) appalled, guessing.
- (C) frightened, curious.
- (D) worried, considering.

6 With which ethnic background/s does Georgia identify?

- (A) Māori and Samoan.
- (B) Māori, Samoan and Tokelauan.
- (C) Samoan and Tokelauan.
- (D) Tokelauan and Māori.

7 Mātauranga Māori refers to a body of knowledge from a Māori perspective (culture, values, traditions, understanding of the natural world, for example). What is the main way Georgia learned mātauranga Māori?

- (A) By going to kōhanga reo.
- (B) By learning in schools with small groups.
- (C) By doing te ao Māori arts.
- (D) By going to kōhanga reo and Te Kura Kaupapa Māori o Ōtepoti (Māori language immersion schools).

8 This article from a New Zealand *School Journal* uses many te reo Māori words that are not translated into English. Why is this?

- (A) The meaning of the words is clear from the context.
- (B) Most of today's New Zealand school students will know what these words mean so they don't need to be translated.
- (C) These words are becoming more common in New Zealand English.
- (D) These words are becoming more common in NZ English and most of today's New Zealand school students will know what these words mean so they don't need to be translated.

ISBN: 9780170499286

TEXT 9

Read the blog below from BLUNT Umbrella NZ's website and answer the questions that follow.

Do BLUNT umbrellas flip inside out?

We answer one of the most commonly asked questions we get about our compact Metro umbrella. Discover how it's designed to handle high winds, why flipping isn't a failure, and what makes BLUNT different from the rest.

Let's be real, flipping inside out is pretty much the universal symbol of an umbrella giving up. **We've all seen it, or lived it, where a strong gust of wind hits and suddenly your umbrella's doing its best impression of a satellite dish.** Not ideal.

So, naturally, one of the most common questions we get asked is:

"Do BLUNT umbrellas flip inside out?"

And we get it. You're investing in quality, so you want to know exactly what you're in for.

So... do they?

Yes, but there's a difference.

Our Metro model, the most compact umbrella in our range, can flip inside out in high winds. But here's the thing, unlike a typical umbrella it won't break. No bent ribs. No snapped spokes. Just a quick pop back into shape and you're good to go.

That's all thanks to our patented Radial Tensioning System (RTS) and flexible frame design. These work together to absorb and distribute pressure without compromising the structure, it's built to bounce back.

Why does it happen?

The BLUNT Metro is designed to be small, light, and easy to carry. Think of it as your everyday go-to. But because of its compact size, it naturally has a bit less resistance to intense wind gusts compared to our larger models like the Classic or Exec.

That's a **trade-off** we make in favour of convenience and portability, but one we balance with serious durability.

We design our umbrellas to handle moments like this. A flip isn't a failure, it's a clever bit of flexibility that lets the umbrella recover, rather than snap under pressure.

Built to recover, not break

We engineer all our umbrellas for resilience. Every model is wind-tested, weatherproof, and built to last. When the weather turns wild, your umbrella should be able to take it. That's why more and more people are choosing the BLUNT Metro as their go-to compact umbrella. Whether you're battling city wind tunnels or sudden downpours, the Metro is designed to handle the chaos and keep you covered.

WHO wrote the text/the source of the text?
WHY was the text written?
WHERE was the text published?
WHAT are the key ideas?
HOW has the text communicated these ideas?

ISBN: 9780170499286

Select (✓) the correct answer to the multiple-choice questions below.

1 What do the letters 'RTS' stand for in the article?

- (A) Responsive Tensioning Structure
- (B) Reinforced Telescopic System
- (C) Radial Tensioning System
- (D) Rapid Twist Support

2 What is one of the most common questions BLUNT receives about their Metro umbrella?

- (A) How long does it last?
- (B) Is it waterproof?
- (C) Does it flip inside out?
- (D) What colours are available?

3 According to the article, what happens when a BLUNT Metro flips inside out?

- (A) It pops back into shape.
- (B) It breaks like a normal umbrella.
- (C) It snaps and becomes unusable.
- (D) It turns into a satellite dish.

4 Why is the BLUNT Metro more likely to flip than other models?

- (A) It has weaker materials.
- (B) It is the most compact umbrella.
- (C) It's not designed for wind.
- (D) It lacks spokes.

5 The Classic or Exec models can be described as what?

- (A) Compact and convenient.
- (B) Designed for more extreme wind.
- (C) Portable and lightweight.
- (D) An everyday umbrella.

6 In the sentence '*That's a **trade-off** we make in favour of convenience and portability, ...*' what is the closest meaning of the word '***trade-off***'?

- (A) a balanced compromise
- (B) an added bonus
- (C) a financial transaction
- (D) a poor decision

7 What does the article suggest about people who often buy cheap umbrellas?

- (A) They are better prepared for storms.
- (B) They care more about colour than quality.
- (C) They enjoy throwing umbrellas away.
- (D) They get frustrated when umbrellas break easily.

8 Which of the following best supports the idea that this article is reliable and trustworthy?

- (A) It uses complicated technical language to sound impressive.
- (B) It never mentions any weaknesses of the product.
- (C) It openly admits the Metro can flip inside out and explains why.
- (D) It guarantees the umbrella will never be damaged.

9 What do the words 'You're investing in quality' suggest?

- (A) You need an investment to buy a BLUNT umbrella.
- (B) BLUNT umbrellas are expensive.
- (C) BLUNT umbrellas are expensive and therefore good quality.
- (D) You should buy a BLUNT umbrella.

Read the information below from Zero Waste Europe and answer the questions that follow.

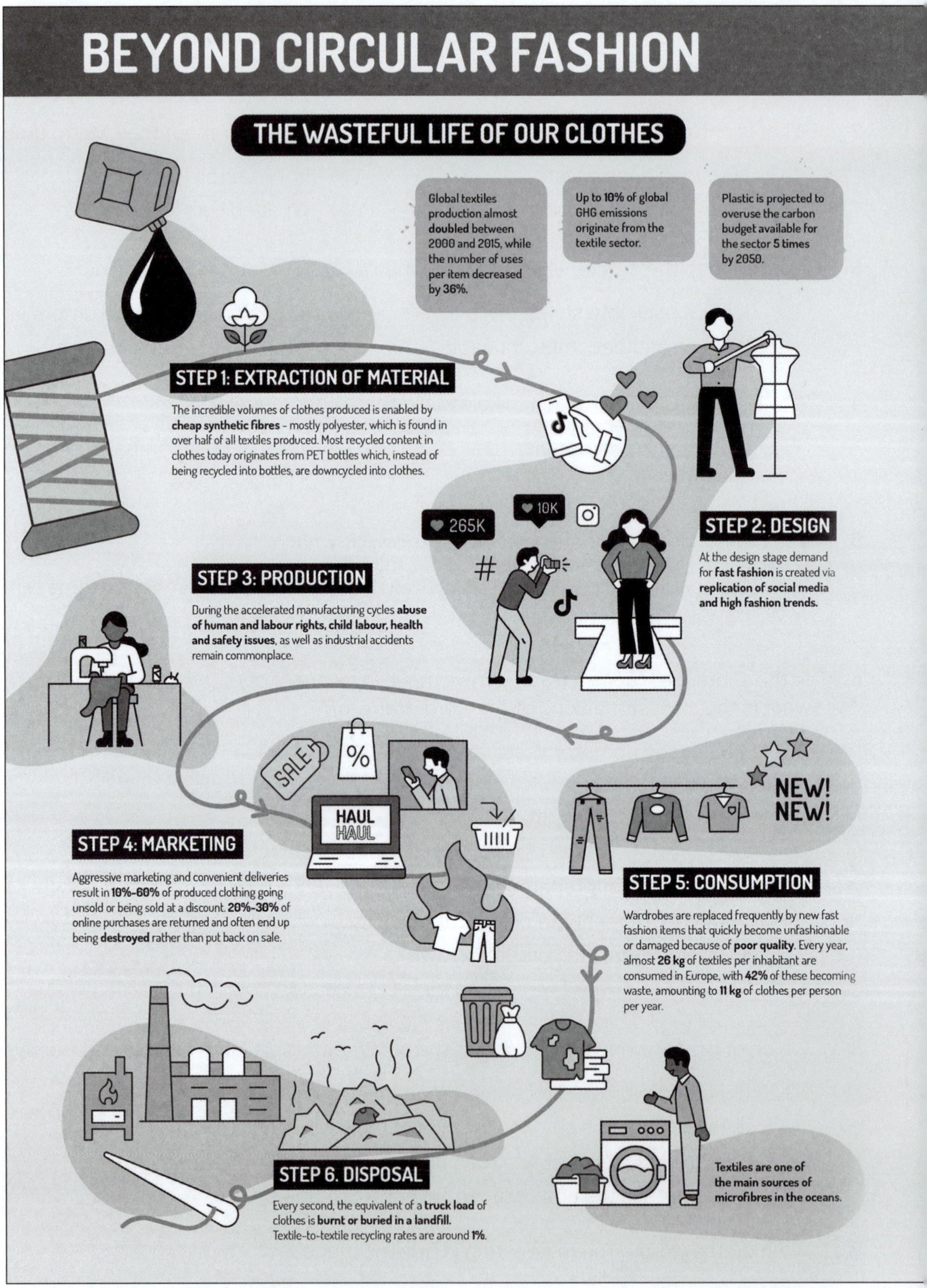

BEYOND CIRCULAR FASHION

THE WASTEFUL LIFE OF OUR CLOTHES

Global textiles production almost **doubled** between 2000 and 2015, while the number of uses per item decreased by **36%**.

Up to **10%** of global GHG emissions originate from the textile sector.

Plastic is projected to overuse the carbon budget available for the sector **5 times** by 2050.

STEP 1: EXTRACTION OF MATERIAL

The incredible volumes of clothes produced is enabled by **cheap synthetic fibres** – mostly polyester, which is found in over half of all textiles produced. Most recycled content in clothes today originates from PET bottles which, instead of being recycled into bottles, are downcycled into clothes.

STEP 2: DESIGN

At the design stage demand for **fast fashion** is created via **replication of social media and high fashion trends.**

265K

10K

#

STEP 3: PRODUCTION

During the accelerated manufacturing cycles **abuse of human and labour rights, child labour, health and safety issues**, as well as industrial accidents remain commonplace.

SALE

%

HAUL
HAUL

STEP 4: MARKETING

Aggressive marketing and convenient deliveries result in **10%-60%** of produced clothing going unsold or being sold at a discount. **20%-30%** of online purchases are returned and often end up being **destroyed** rather than put back on sale.

NEW!
NEW!

STEP 5: CONSUMPTION

Wardrobes are replaced frequently by new fast fashion items that quickly become unfashionable or damaged because of **poor quality**. Every year, almost **26 kg** of textiles per inhabitant are consumed in Europe, with **42%** of these becoming waste, amounting to **11 kg** of clothes per person per year.

Textiles are one of the main sources of microfibres in the oceans.

STEP 6. DISPOSAL

Every second, the equivalent of a **truck load** of clothes is **burnt or buried in a landfill.** Textile-to-textile recycling rates are around **1%**.

ISBN: 9780170499286

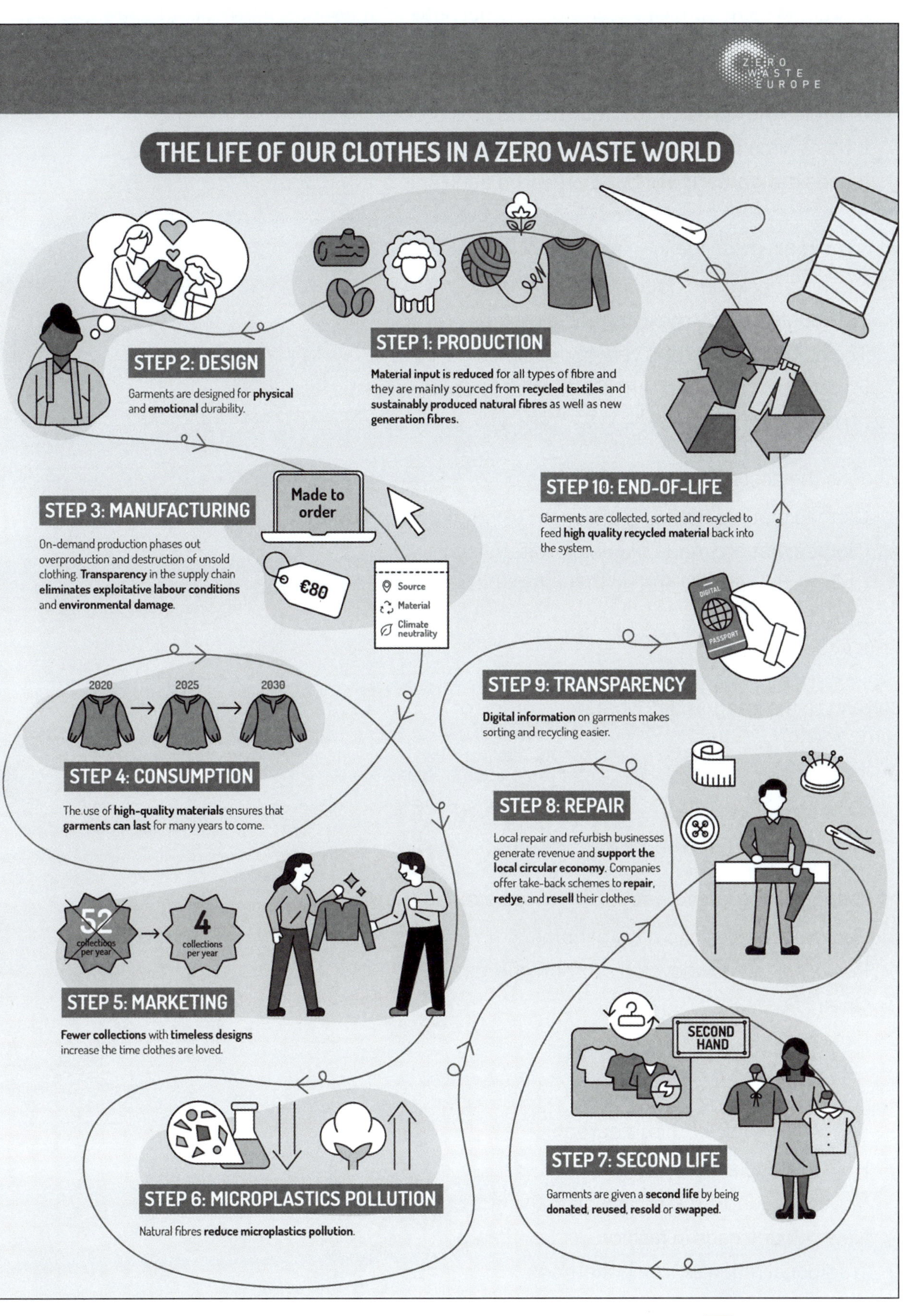

STOP AND THINK

WHO wrote the text/the source of the text?
WHY was the text written?
WHERE was the text published?
WHAT are the key ideas?
HOW has the text communicated these ideas?

Select (✓) the correct answer to the multiple-choice questions below.

1 The infographic on the previous spread is divided into two sections. How does the graphic show this?

- (A) It is about waste on one side and recycling on the other.
- (B) It divides the spread into two with a vertical broken line.
- (C) It has a circular line with arrows on both sides.
- (D) It uses the words 'life of our clothes' on each side.

2 What is the main message in this infographic?

- (A) Clothing designers do a good job for us.
- (B) We should recycle our synthetic clothing.
- (C) The clothing industry is very complex.
- (D) People must demand that the clothing industry creates less waste.

3 What does the poster suggest is 'fast fashion'?

- (A) Clothes that are made for a current trend to be used briefly.
- (B) Clothes that are made of cheap materials.
- (C) Clothes that mostly end up in the trash.
- (D) All of the above.

4 According to the infographic, what percentage of clothes purchased each year in Europe become waste?

- (A) 18%
- (B) 60%
- (C) 42%
- (D) 75%

5 What does the infographic want clothing to be made from?

- (A) Recycled textiles and natural fibres.
- (B) Recycled and downcycled synthetic fibres.
- (C) Cheap fibres.
- (D) Expensive recycled fabrics.

6 What is the main topic of this infographic?

- (A) How to recycle food waste.
- (B) Moving beyond circular fashion in the clothing industry.
- (C) New colour trends in fashion.
- (D) Traditional manufacturing methods.

ISBN: 9780170499286

7 What is the purpose of placing the two diagrams side-by-side in the infographic?

- (A) To show what materials are the most popular.
- (B) To compare the current fashion system with a more sustainable one.
- (C) To divide the information by region.
- (D) To focus only on the recycling process.

8 What is the infographic encouraging fashion companies to do?

- (A) Use cheaper materials.
- (B) Focus only on recycling.
- (C) Export their waste overseas.
- (D) Create fewer products and use resources wisely.

9 Look at the graphics for STEP 2: DESIGN (left section). What do the graphics suggest?

- (A) Taking photographs is a sales technique.
- (B) Models are female.
- (C) Liking clothing on social media platforms creates high demand.
- (D) Fast fashion is good.

10 Look at STEP 3: PRODUCTION (left section). What is this suggesting is a negative effect of demand for fast fashion?

- (A) People making these clothes have to work hard.
- (B) Places where these clothes are made are too busy.
- (C) Lots of boring jobs are created by the fashion industry.
- (D) People making these clothes could be unsafe.

11 What does the phrase 'beyond circular' imply in the context of fashion?

- (A) That the industry should do more than just recycle.
- (B) That circular systems are bad.
- (C) That designers should use only natural fibres.
- (D) That fast fashion supports recycling.

12 How does the thread line on each side of the infographic support the clothing cycle idea?

- (A) The arrows show it's about sewing to make clothing.
- (B) The arrows show a top to bottom, from make to throw away, process on the wasteful side.
- (C) The arrows show a circle linking STEP 10 to STEP 1, from end to producing, on the zero waste side.
- (D) Both B and C.

Read the article below from the science magazine *Cosmos* and answer the questions that follow.

ZEBRAS OF THE FISH WORLD USE STRIPES TO DAZZLE

Black and white markings cause predator confusion

Zebras aren't the only animal using black and white stripes to dazzle predators on the hunt for a tasty meal.

According to new research, the humbug damselfish – a species of fish that lives in coral reefs throughout the tropical waters of the Indo-Pacific region – also uses motion dazzle as a defence strategy.

The clever coral-dwelling fish might even change their behaviour to protect themselves from predators, depending on the striped patterns perceived around them.

"Our findings show that humbug damselfish **adapt** their behaviour based on their environment," says Dr Louise Tosetto of Australia's Macquarie University.

"In their natural habitat, when they encounter backgrounds resembling their own striped patterns, like branching corals, they tend to move closer and reduce their movement. This likely helps them **blend in** and stay hidden from predators."

Though camouflage is well known for helping prey avoid the attention of predators, it can also help predators sneak up on their prey.

"When feeding outside the coral colony, where camouflage is less effective, [humbug damselfish] increase their movement and rely more on the confusing effects of their stripes, known as **motion dazzle**," says Tosetto.

Motion dazzle protects moving prey by distracting predators through visual illusions, like the repetitive colour patterns of stripes, bands, and zig-zags. The moving stripey patterns of herding zebras makes it difficult for predators to work out the speed, distance, and direction of individual animals.

The researchers filmed humbug damselfish fishtanks with various striped backgrounds to study how they might affect the fish's ability to confuse predators.

They used anatomical data from the retinas of humbugs to understand how clearly the fish might perceive these differently striped patterns and used computer models to simulate how predators would perceive their movements.

Senior author Dr Laura Ryan, also from Macquarie, says the findings show these fish have complex anti-predator strategies.

"This is an essential baseline study that provides new insights into the motion dazzle phenomenon," says Ryan.

STOP AND THINK

WHO wrote the text/the source of the text?
WHY was the text written?
WHERE was the text published?
WHAT are the key ideas?
HOW has the text communicated these ideas?

ISBN: 9780170499286

Select (✓) the correct answer to the multiple-choice questions below.

1 Where do most humbug damselfish live?

- (A) Deep ocean trenches.
- (B) Freshwater lakes.
- (C) Coral reefs in tropical Indo-Pacific waters.
- (D) Antarctic waters.

2 What do the black and white stripes help the fish do?

- (A) Swim faster.
- (B) Confuse predators.
- (C) Attract mates.
- (D) See better.

3 What is '***motion dazzle***'?

- (A) A way to catch prey quickly.
- (B) A method for hiding behind rocks.
- (C) A way predators freeze their prey.
- (D) A confusing effect caused by moving stripes.

4 According to the article, how do humbug damselfish behave when near striped coral?

- (A) They move closer and reduce movement.
- (B) They swim away quickly.
- (C) They flash their stripes.
- (D) They chase predators.

5 Why do the fish increase movement when they're outside the coral colony?

- (A) To make themselves look bigger.
- (B) To signal to other fish.
- (C) To swim away from predators.
- (D) To use motion dazzle more effectively to distract predators.

6 What is the main purpose of this article?

- (A) To make people want pet damselfish.
- (B) To explain how some animals use stripes to avoid predators.
- (C) To describe how coral reefs are formed.
- (D) To argue that zebras and fish are closely related.

7 What does the phrase '**adapt their behaviour**' most likely mean in this sentence?

> *'Our findings show that humbug damselfish **adapt their behaviour** based on their environment.'*

- (A) Ignore their surroundings.
- (B) Copy other animals exactly.
- (C) Change or adjust to fit different conditions.
- (D) Move away from danger.

8 Which word or words could you use instead of '**blend in**' in this sentence without changing the meaning?

> *'This likely helps them **blend in** and stay hidden from predators.'*

- (A) stand out
- (B) separate
- (C) hide
- (D) camouflage

TEXT 12 Read the extract of an interview below from 1news.co.nz and answer the questions that follow.

The story behind the popular New Zealand fashion label YOUKNOW

by Fiona Connor

What does it take to turn an idea into a successful business? Fiona Connor chats to Joe Webb, business owner, about the challenges and the successes.

"You know" was once a phrase used in a positive way by Joe Webb and a group of his friends to show support. He liked using it so much that one day in 2017 he got a mate to print it on a T-shirt.

Webb posted a picture of it on social media, and pretty quickly he found himself with a business.

With a double major in IT and business management, he jumped right in to creating something of his own, and now has a whole range of clothes under his label YOUKNOW.

What did it take to get started?

It was a side hustle for the first year or two, I was working full time and also had a year overseas. I funded it out of my income, no investors. There was no chance I could have funded it without full-time working and then doing extras on the side to fund this new venture.

How many designs did you start with and how did you go about getting your first line manufactured?

T-shirts quickly led to hoodies which are still our most popular item. In the first year or so I did the screen printing myself after work then dispatched them too. Then my partner Aïda and I went overseas. We organised a New Zealand company to produce the product and dispatch it which kept the brand going. Then when we came back after a year working in business development I decided to commit full time to YOUKNOW.

What considerations do you have to give to entering the fashion industry?

We worked hard on getting the right styles/cuts and look and equally on finding the best partners to manufacture and fulfil. We are big on relationships and being really open and honest about what we are doing. We have established some great partner relationships based on trust and honesty.

A big part of YOUKNOW is the community – which means we had to cater to all shapes and sizes and did not want to make a product which people felt they could not wear. Our **mantra** is Confident, Comfortable and Community Driven which essentially means that we want you to feel confident and comfortable in our garments no matter what age, gender or race you are.

What are some of the biggest lessons that others can learn from?

Committing to anything gives you the best chance of success, you can't be half baked and expect a good cake. Honesty and **transparency** is fundamental, success is based on trusted relationships again in whatever you do, never compromise those values because even if the other party doesn't know, you do and it will eat away at you. Expect to work really hard all the time.

Another one would be to work smart not hard – which is super cliché. People forget that your mates and community are the ones that are there for you and if you are at home and not seeing them, they may forget about you.

Also, be aware of becoming arrogant and only ever talking about what you do, you may be consumed by it but others aren't – in fact, make a point not to. Always think about the next thing and look at diversifying as much as possible without losing focus. Keep a broad network to stay in touch and if you keep thinking about a business idea or career path – do it.

The worst that can happen is it fails and you go back to your nine to five.

STOP AND THINK

WHO wrote the text/the source of the text?
WHY was the text written?
WHERE was the text published?
WHAT are the key ideas?
HOW has the text communicated these ideas?

 ISBN: 9780170499286

Select (✓) the correct answer to the multiple-choice questions below.

1 What phrase did Joe Webb originally print on a T-shirt?

- (A) Y'know
- (B) YOUKNOW clothing
- (C) You know
- (D) Younow

2 What did Joe Webb do before committing to YOUKNOW full time?

- (A) He worked in a full-time job and lived overseas.
- (B) He worked in social media.
- (C) He was a full-time investor.
- (D) He started the brand at university.

3 What does the word '**mantra**' most likely mean in this phrase?

*'Our **mantra** is Confident, Comfortable and Community Driven ...'*

- (A) A product line.
- (B) A guiding belief or motto.
- (C) A discount code.
- (D) A social media post.

4 Which word could best replace '**transparency**' in this phrase?

*'Honesty and **transparency** is fundamental, ...'*

- (A) confusion
- (B) secretiveness
- (C) shininess
- (D) openness

5 What can we assume about how Joe Webb views success?

- (A) It comes mainly from being lucky.
- (B) It's only about selling lots of products.
- (C) It depends on hard work and strong relationships.
- (D) It's easier if you copy others on TikTok.

6 How is the article structured to make it easy to read?

- (A) It's written as an article.
- (B) It uses questions and answers in an interview format.
- (C) It's written as a fictional story.
- (D) It uses a timeline of events.

7 What makes this article feel more trustworthy?

- (A) It quotes the business owner directly.
- (B) It uses technical fashion terms.
- (C) It uses emojis and slang.
- (D) It includes product ads.

TEXT 13

Read the information below adapted from the *New Zealand Herald* website. Then answer the questions that follow.

Discussing scam safety with your kids

In partnership with ASB

You don't have to be a grown-up to fall for an online scam.

ASB Bank's digital fraud expert Alex Hinde says: "We expect scammers to target older people who frequently shop and pay bills online. Yet children and teenagers are also at risk."

Today's young people have grown up with smartphones, tablets and the internet. But when it comes to online fraud, they are as vulnerable as adults. In some ways, their familiarity with technology makes them even more susceptible.

"Children can be naive, but they are also **desensitised** to online risk," Hinde says. "Older people know there's a risk with online transactions. Younger people grew up with them, so often don't necessarily stay alert or take special care."

That's why it's important to talk about online safety early.

Many scams targeting children mirror those aimed at adults, but they are adapted for a younger audience.

How parents and caregivers can help

Hinde recommends these steps to help protect your children or teenagers when they're online:

- Encourage open communication – Make sure they feel safe coming to you if something doesn't seem right.
- Know the platforms – Understand what social media and websites your kids use and what they share.
- Talk about online risks – Explain the dangers of posting their personal information and strangers who ask for money or photos. Help them recognise suspicious behaviour.
- Monitor transactions – If they want to buy something online, have them check with you first. Avoid sharing your card details with them.
- Use security tools – Consider parental controls or monitoring software. Many schools already use similar technology.
- Check out netsafe.org.nz for more information on keeping kids safe.

Advice for children and teenagers

- Be wary of strangers on the internet who ask for photos or money.
- Don't respond to bullying.
- Talk to your parents, teacher or an adult that you know and trust if someone online is making you feel uncomfortable. You can also chat to Youthline – call 0800 37 66 33, text 234, or chat online at youthline.co.nz.
- Save evidence: screenshots, usernames and URLs. Block, unfriend and report any incidents.
- If you feel very unsafe, call Police on 111.

Call your bank immediately if you think your card or banking details have been compromised. For more information that can help you and your family stay safe from scams, head to asb.co.nz/scamhub.

STOP AND THINK

WHO wrote the text/the source of the text?
WHY was the text written?
WHERE was the text published?
WHAT are the key ideas?
HOW has the text communicated these ideas?

ISBN: 9780170499286

Select (✓) the correct answer to the multiple-choice questions below.

1 What kind of advice does this article give?

- (A) How to save money at ASB.
- (B) Why the internet is dangerous.
- (C) How to use internet banking
- (D) How to keep children safe from online scams.

2 Why does the writer use bullet points in this article?

- (A) To give opinions.
- (B) To make advice easy to read and follow.
- (C) To show quotes from children.
- (D) To explain social media apps.

3 What does the phrase 'In partnership with ASB' suggest about the article?

- (A) It's promoting Youthline services.
- (B) It's only for ASB customers.
- (C) It was created with support from ASB.
- (D) It was made by partners of the ASB.

4 Why is the sentence '***You don't have to be a grown-up to fall for an online scam.***' written in **bold,** blue and *italics*?

- (A) To show it is untrue.
- (B) To act as a title.
- (C) To highlight an expert quote.
- (D) To grab attention and highlight the key message.

5 What does the word '**desensitised**' most likely mean in this sentence?

'Children can be naive, but they are also ***desensitised*** *to online risk.'*

- (A) Less aware or concerned about risk.
- (B) More likely to report danger.
- (C) Less experienced online.
- (D) Angry about scams.

6 What does the writer believe about children and scams?

- (A) They are better at spotting them than adults.
- (B) They're too young to understand risk.
- (C) They can be targeted just like adults.
- (D) They should be left to manage scams alone.

7 Why are there links to other websites like *netsafe.org.nz* or *youthline.co.nz*?

- (A) To promote popular social media.
- (B) To trick readers into clicking.
- (C) To show where the article was copied from.
- (D) To give readers access to more trusted help and advice.

8 Why can the reader trust the information in this article?

- (A) It tells you what to buy.
- (B) It includes made-up stories.
- (C) It quotes experts and links to trusted organisations.
- (D) It was posted on social media.

Read the tourism reviews below and answer the questions that follow.

Text A: Reviews of Ocean Spirit Dolphin Encounter

Amira L. – Mum of Two, Christchurch
1 month ago
We did the watching tour with our kids (3 and 6), and it was unforgettable. The dolphins were everywhere and so playful! Staff were great with children, and the views were stunning. A perfect family adventure without getting wet!

Helen T. – Retired Teacher, Wellington
3 months ago
A dream come true! At 67, I was nervous, but the team was kind and helpful. The winter gear kept me warm, and seeing the dolphins so close was magical. Even staying near the boat gave amazing views. Highly recommend – just take seasickness meds if you're unsure.

Jayden R. – Backpacker from the UK
9 months ago
Swimming with so many dolphins was unreal – like being in a nature documentary! But I got seasick halfway through and missed a lot. Definitely take medication beforehand. Amazing wildlife, but not fun if you're queasy.

Text B: Reviews of Blue Horizon Kayaks

Lisa M. – Adventure Tourist, Auckland
3 weeks ago
Absolutely loved the sunset kayaking! The calm water and stunning views of the Kaikōura ranges made it unforgettable. We even saw fur seals playing right beside us and even spotted a few dolphins in the distance. The guide was knowledgeable and friendly. Highly recommend for anyone wanting a peaceful but exciting marine experience.

Tom S. – Dad, Christchurch
6 months ago
I was really disappointed we couldn't join the family kayaking tour as my youngest is only 2. We'd been looking forward to a chance to see the wildlife together, but their minimum age policy means we had to sit this one out. I understand safety is important, but a bit more flexibility or options for younger kids would be great.

Emily R. – Solo Traveller, Wellington
1 year ago
I did a private kayaking tour last winter and it was incredible. The water was chilly but the views were **spectacular**, and I even caught sight of migrating humpback whales! The kayak was stable and the guide made sure I was comfortable and safe. The only minor downside was the early start in winter, but totally worth it.

Mark D. – Local Resident, Kaikōura
3 years ago
As a local, I love how Blue Horizon Kayaks shows visitors the beauty of our marine life. I've done several tours with them over the years, and the wildlife encounters never get old. The seals and penguins are always playful, and the guides are passionate and knowledgeable. A genuine Kiwi experience every time!

STOP AND THINK

WHO wrote the text/the source of the text?
WHY was the text written?
WHERE was the text published?
WHAT are the key ideas?
HOW has the text communicated these ideas?

ISBN: 9780170499286

Select (✓) the correct answer to the multiple-choice questions below.

1 Which activity did Lisa M. enjoy most on her tour?

- (A) Swimming with dolphins.
- (B) Sunset kayaking.
- (C) Snorkelling with seals.
- (D) Watching penguins from the shore.

2 What was Tom S.'s main reason for disappointment?

- (A) The weather was too cold for kayaking.
- (B) The guides were unhelpful.
- (C) The tour was cancelled due to low numbers.
- (D) His child was too young to join the family kayaking tour.

3 According to Emily R., what wildlife did she see on her winter kayaking tour?

- (A) Dusky dolphins and penguins.
- (B) New Zealand fur seals.
- (C) Humpback whales.
- (D) Bottlenose dolphins.

4 What common feature do both Amira L. and Helen T. mention in their reviews?

- (A) The cold water temperature.
- (B) The friendly and supportive staff.
- (C) Difficulty swimming with dolphins.
- (D) Seeing penguins on the tour.

5 Which of these reviews includes a suggestion related to preparation for seasickness?

- (A) Jayden R.
- (B) Tom S.
- (C) Emily R.
- (D) Mark D.

6 Which review is an example of a disappointed customer?

- (A) Helen T.
- (B) Tom S.
- (C) Amira L.
- (D) Mark D.

7 Which is the best replacement for the word '**spectacular**' in the sentence below?

*'The water was chilly but the views were **spectacular**,
and I even caught sight of migrating humpback whales!'*

- (A) spectacle
- (B) unusual
- (C) impressive
- (D) strange

8 How might the age of some reviews affect their reliability for someone planning a tour today?

- (A) Newer reviews are less reliable because people haven't had time to reflect on their experience.
- (B) Older reviews are always more reliable because they have stood the test of time.
- (C) The age of a review doesn't affect its reliability at all.
- (D) Older reviews might be less reliable because tour details, staff, or wildlife encounters could have changed over time.

9 Why is it good to look at reviews before booking an experience/trip?

- (A) To learn about other people's experiences and know what to expect.
- (B) To make sure the experience is the cheapest option available.
- (C) Because reviews always guarantee you will have a perfect time.
- (D) So you can avoid reading the company's official information.

ISBN: 9780170499286

Read the information below from Diabetes New Zealand's pamphlet and website. Answer the questions that follow.

Text A

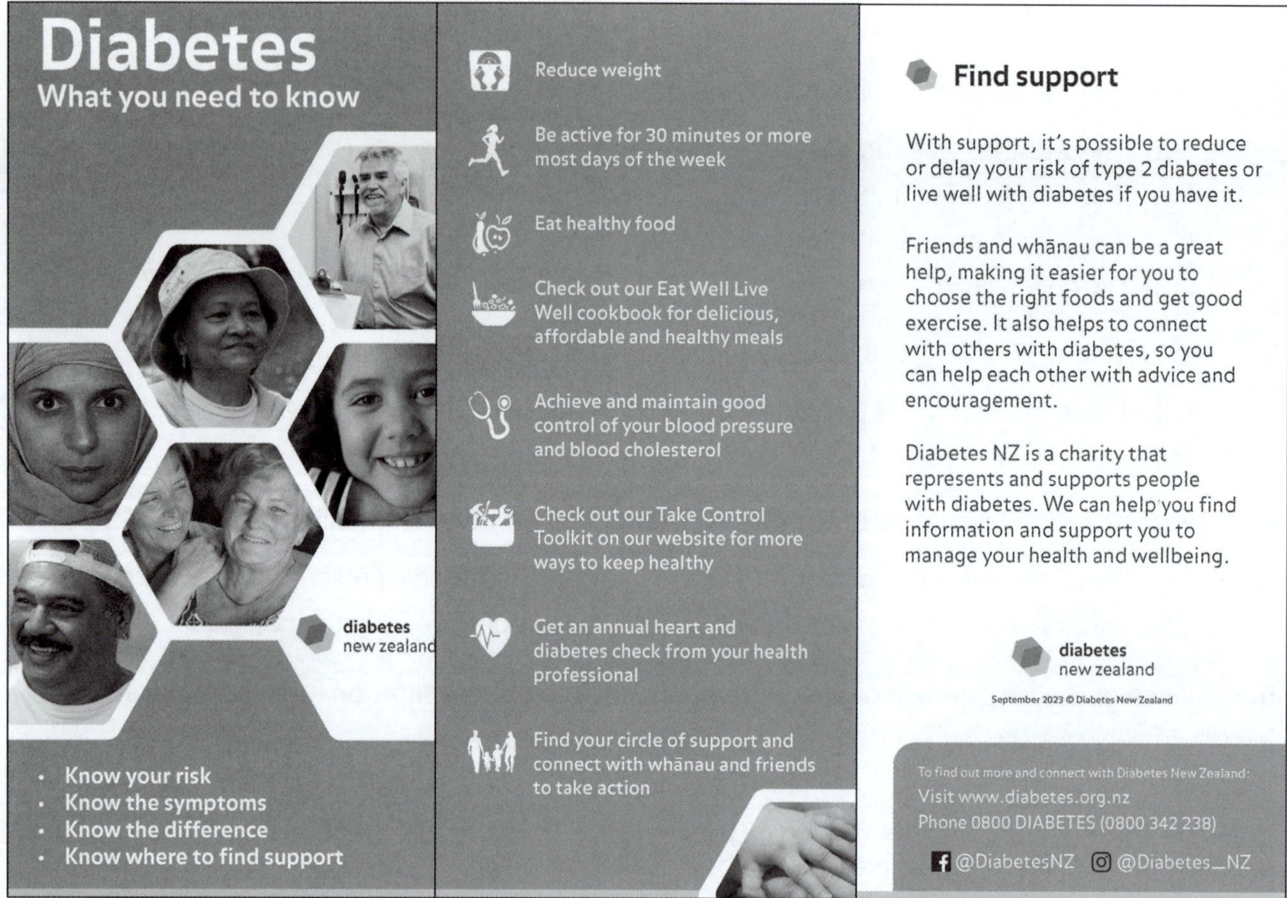

Text B

Liam's story

We have been helping tamariki in Aotearoa New Zealand learn to live well with diabetes with the help of Jerry the Bear for the past eight years. Since launching in November 2017, Jerry the Bear has been included in our 'Brave Bear packs', which get sent to children aged 4–10 years all over the motu.

As well as the bear himself, the accompanying smartphone app supports tamariki to discover how they can still play with their friends, take part in activities and sports and enjoy life to the full – all while learning how to manage their diabetes.

One brave type 1 warrior Liam received a Brave Bear pack and his mum Hilary has shared how things have been going since Jerry came to live with them!

"Liam loves his Jerry Bear. He has even made some injection pens out of Lego! Liam gives Jerry an injection in his tummy every time I give him an insulin injection. He is proud to be able to look after Jerry. He always holds Jerry when he has his insulin. Jerry has already been a great friend and I'm sure he will be for years to come!"

Our free Jerry Bear programme is made possible with funding we receive from grants as well as generous donations from charities, clubs and incredible members of the public. If you would like to learn more, or find out how to order one for a child in your life, visit our dedicated Brave Bear page: Diabetes New Zealand

ISBN: 9780170499286

Select (✓) the correct answer to the multiple-choice questions below.

1 What is the main reason why the pamphlet uses photographs of real people?

- (A) To show people with diabetes smile a lot.
- (B) To make the pamphlet look friendly.
- (C) To suggest anyone of any age or ethnicity can have diabetes.
- (D) To suggest Diabetes NZ is a charity.

STOP AND THINK

WHO wrote the text/the source of the text?
WHY was the text written?
WHERE was the text published?
WHAT are the key ideas?
HOW has the text communicated these ideas?

2 What three useful self-help ideas mentioned in the central column of the pamphlet are repeated in the right column?

- (A) Lose weight, eat healthy food, control blood pressure.
- (B) Eat good food, connect with friends and whānau, exercise regularly.
- (C) Get the cookbook, check the website, get a heart check.
- (D) Go running, eat delicious food, talk to others with diabetes.

3 What are the best two ways a person could contact Diabetes NZ?

- (A) Through the website and the internet.
- (B) By using the telephone or asking a friend.
- (C) Via Facebook and Instagram.
- (D) By visiting the website or phoning the freephone number.

4 When was Jerry Bear first sent to children with diabetes?

- (A) Since November.
- (B) In 2017.
- (C) Eight years ago.
- (D) 4–10 years ago.

5 How does the writing suggest Jerry Bear helps young children who have diabetes?

- (A) He gets an injection when the child does.
- (B) The children can hold the bear when they get an injection.
- (C) Jerry Bear feels like a good friend who is sharing their experiences.
- (D) Jerry is a free gift.

6 Why does the pamphlet have icons in the central column?

- (A) To visually represent each key health action and make the information easier to understand.
- (B) To make the brochure look more colourful and decorative.
- (C) To fill up space so the page doesn't look empty.
- (D) To show examples of medical tools used for diabetes.

7 What ideas about living with diabetes do both texts offer?

- (A) That diabetes requires lots of medical help.
- (B) That diabetes means completely changing your life.
- (C) That diabetes affects children more than adults.
- (D) That diabetes should not stop a person from living their life well.

8 These two texts are on a similar topic but they are aimed at different audiences. Choose the answer that best describes these two audiences.

- (A) The pamphlet is for any person who has diabetes, the webpage is for children only.
- (B) The webpage is a story for anyone and the pamphlet is facts for diabetics.
- (C) The webpage is for parents/caregivers of small children but the pamphlet is for anyone who is affected by diabetes.
- (D) The pamphlet is advice for caregivers and the webpage is a story for little children and their family.

TEXT 16 A and B

Read the extracts below from a newspaper article in the *Northern Advocate* and the novel *Cuz* by Liz Van der Laarse. Answer the questions that follow.

Text A

Home / Northern Advocate

Far North author weaves Māori survival methods into kids' book

A story of survival and grief is the latest offering from Northland author Liz Van der Laarse, her first to be published in 15 years.

Cuz is about two 14-year-old cousins forced to fend for themselves in the West Coast wilderness.

The cousins, Huia and River, rely on traditional methods of tikanga Māori methods of survival Huia has learnt from her whānau. Van der Laarse decided to write stories with Māori characters after discovering just how few were available.

Cuz not only features main characters who are Māori, but also "quite a bit" of te reo and also tikanga Māori.

"I'd like to see more te reo just in everyday use, and also to make people more aware of tikanga Māori. Those two things are important to me."

Van der Laarse, who has lived in the Far North for more than 40 years, has already written two junior fiction books – *Trouble Patch* and *Not Even*.

Both books, like *Cuz*, feature main characters who are Māori.

Not Even was placed on the Storylines Notable Book List in 2003 in the Junior Fiction category.

Van der Laarse has taught throughout the district, starting as a first-year teacher in Kāeo.

All her books were initially written with intermediate-age kids in mind – the age group she taught – although the characters are slightly older and her books have been read by children aged 10 to 15.

All three of her books are written to keep kids' attention.

"I wanted to write books that were fast-paced, with lots of action. All three books are like that."

The idea for her latest novel came about largely because of Van der Laarse's hobby – tramping.

"I've had over 20 years' tramping experience. My husband and I go to the South Island every year, really."

When Van der Laarse's husband pointed out an edible plant on one of their tramping trips, it sparked the idea for a survival story.

ISBN: 9780170499286

Text B

Cuz

Huia smiled. She hugged her arms lightly across her chest. "We need a fire ... I get so cold sitting around. My clothes aren't even properly dry yet."

"What did Nan teach you? She told me that story once. Which tree holds the seeds of fire?"

"Kaikōmako."

"Is it here?"

Huia squinted at the forest surrounding the clearing. "Dunno. Go and get heaps of different leaves ... and I'll have a look."

River saw the forest was full of all kinds of plants. He collected thick and shiny leaves, ragged and fragile ones, others hairy and leathery. Huia picked out a soft leaf with zigzag edges.

"Is that kaikō ... something?" River asked.

"Kaikōmako. Nah, this is māhoe. We need it too .... it's the soft wood. Kaikōmako is the hard one."

"Did I get that?"

Huia held up leathery leaves shaped like a duck's feet. "Ae."

"Yeah? Awesome." He looked back into the forest. His smile disappeared. "Far, how am I going to find them again?"

"Take the two leaves with you, cuz. Māhoe's bark is white ... look for that ... the young kaikōmako plants are a crazy pile of thin-as branches ... the mother tree will be near it. And grab some dry lichen too. Or dried leaves."

"Eh?"

"For fire starters."

River searched among the mossy trees, through tangles of vines and scratchy ferns. His eyes rested on an old grey tree. He grinned. It had the duck-feet leaves. River grabbed a broken branch wedged in the tree. By the edge of the clearing, a white-barked tree stood out against the greens. Māhoe.

"These them?" He held the two branches out to Huia.

Her blue fingers grasped the wood. "Ae, fulla." She grinned up at him.

STOP AND THINK

WHO wrote the text/the source of the text?
WHY was the text written?
WHERE was the text published?
WHAT are the key ideas?
HOW has the text communicated these ideas?

Select (✓) the correct answer to the multiple-choice questions below.

1 What is *Cuz* mainly about?

- (A) A family holiday in the South Island.
- (B) A school trip that goes wrong.
- (C) Two cousins surviving in the wilderness.
- (D) A group of students exploring the South Island.

2 What inspired Liz Van der Laarse to write *Cuz*?

- (A) Her desire to teach outdoor safety in schools.
- (B) Her tramping trips and knowledge of edible plants.
- (C) Her experiences as a nurse in rural New Zealand.
- (D) Her childhood growing up on the West Coast.

3 According to the article, who are Van der Laarse's books written for?

- (A) Preschool readers.
- (B) University students.
- (C) Intermediate-aged children.
- (D) Teachers and parents.

4 Why does Huia ask River to collect lots of different leaves at first?

- (A) To confuse him.
- (B) So she can use them for medicine.
- (C) To test his bush knowledge.
- (D) So she can identify the right ones.

5 Why did Van der Laarse decide to include Māori characters in her books?

- (A) Because she realised there were very few books with Māori characters.
- (B) Because she was commissioned to do so.
- (C) Because all her students were Māori.
- (D) Because her books were originally written in te reo.

6 In the extract from *Cuz*, how does Huia show her knowledge of traditional survival skills?

- (A) She takes him to useful trees.
- (B) She tells River to follow his instincts like their tūpuna.
- (C) She gives River detailed instructions about fire-starting plants.
- (D) She shows River how to navigate using the stars.

7 How does the *Cuz* extract reflect Liz Van der Laarse's goal of promoting tikanga Māori?

- (A) By showing how Huia and River fend for themselves in the bush.
- (B) By describing how Huia wants to return to the city.
- (C) By showing Huia using Māori plant names and traditional survival skills.
- (D) By using English names for plants to make the story more accessible.

8 What is a shared idea in both the article and the *Cuz* extract?

- (A) Both show how survival depends on modern technology.
- (B) Both explain the science behind fire-making methods.
- (C) Both describe the dangers of getting lost in the forest.
- (D) Both highlight the role of whānau in passing on knowledge.

9 What major aim, stated in the author's interview, is shown in the extract from the novel?

- (A) It is set in New Zealand.
- (B) It uses words in te reo and shows tikanga Māori.
- (C) It is about the bush in the South Island.
- (D) It is written for young readers.

ISBN: 9780170499286

Let's be accurate

Kia tika tātou

To achieve the Literacy Writing assessment, you must be able to write with a reasonable level of accuracy.

- You must be able to spell common words accurately.
- You must be able to use basic punctuation marks properly.
- You must be able to write in complete sentences.

The Literacy Writing assessment will check that you are able to use:

- essential punctuation: capital letters and full stops.
- other punctuation marks: comma, exclamation mark, question mark, speech marks.
- the apostrophe for contracted verbs and possession.
- correct spelling.

You know something about all of these things. Here, we are going to remind you of the basic skills you need for this assessment.

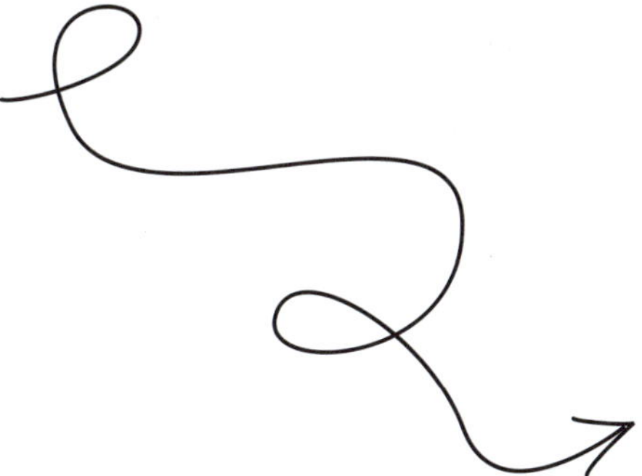

ISBN: 9780170499286

Punctuation – the basics

The capital letter

1 Sentences always start with a capital letter.

For example: **M**y auntie lives on my street.

2 A proper noun is the specific name of a person, place or thing and it needs a capital letter.

For example: **M**y auntie, **M**illie, likes to go to the cafe called **M**ilkshed.

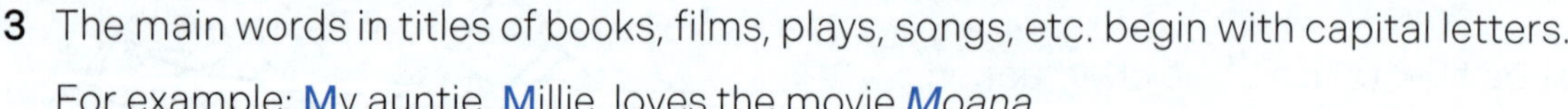

3 The main words in titles of books, films, plays, songs, etc. begin with capital letters.

For example: **M**y auntie, **M**illie, loves the movie *Moana*.

4 Capital letters begin the first word inside speech marks.

For example: **M**y auntie, **M**illie, said, '**L**et's go to the **M**ilkshed for lunch.'

'I' or 'i'?
'I' is the personal pronoun. It is **always** a capital letter.
For example: **I** asked **M**um if **I** could go to the mall and she said that **I** could.

YOUR TURN

Overwrite the words in each sentence that need a capital letter.

1 in november we are going to sydney to see our old friend barney.
(You will need 4 of them.)

2 freddy and fergus flew down to wellington to go to te papa.
(You will need 5 of them.)

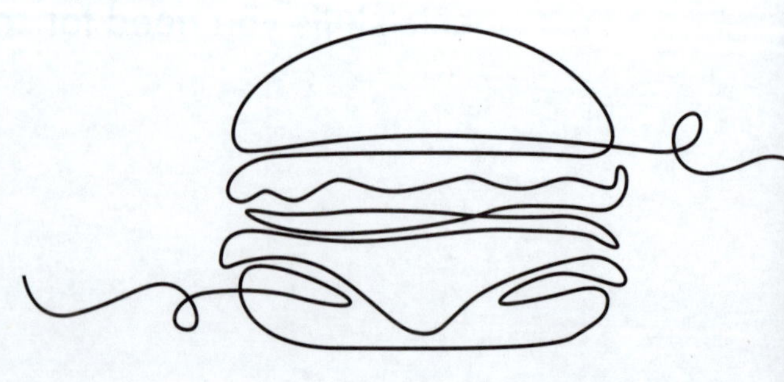

3 my brother ashton hates hamburgers, but i love them.
(You will need 3 of them.)

4 i asked for a lego set for my Birthday because I love lego.
(You will need to add 3 and remove 1 of them.)

5 we're going snowboarding in taranaki on july 17th.
(You will need 3 of them.)

 ISBN: 9780170499286

The full stop (.)

Sentences always end with a full stop.

For example: The pear tree produces tasty pears in autumn.

YOUR TURN

Without changing the order of the words, add the missing capital letters and full stops.

1 this is a really easy chocolate cake recipe it truly tastes of chocolate it keeps for up to five days. *(Make 3 sentences.)*

2 venus is the second planet from the Sun it is similar in size to Earth and it is the hottest planet in our solar system Venus is named after the Roman goddess of love and beauty. *(Make 3 sentences.)*

3 my room is extremely tidy my sister's room is not she has a desk with a volcano of books on top of it. *(Make 3 sentences.)*

4 i love living in the city where there's so much to do every day the shops and the cafes and the cinemas are always open the city is a great place to live for someone like me. *(Make 3 sentences.)*

5 i go to the skatepark every afternoon after school it's the best place for me to practise for hours if my mate joe is around he comes too. *(Make 3 sentences.)*

The question mark (?)

A question mark is placed at the end of a sentence that asks a direct question.

For example:

- Are you hungry?
- Will you pay for my ticket?
- Shall we go to the game together?

However, the sentences below are not direct questions. They do not need a question mark.

- My grandma always asks if I am hungry.
- Tom asked me if I would pay for his ticket.
- Dad asked us if we should go to the game together.

Because the question mark behaves like a full stop when it is at the end of a sentence, you do not need a full stop as well. Look carefully and you will see the question mark includes a full stop.

If the question mark is inside speech marks, it may not be followed by a capital letter if it is not the end of the sentence.

For example:
'Do you want an ice cream?' asked Mum.
'Have you done your homework?' questioned the teacher.

YOUR TURN

Put a question mark into any of these sentences that need one.

1 'Will you come to the movie tomorrow' asked Jill.

2 I'm going to the park. Do you want to come with me.

3 Our teacher always asks us if we're ready to start the lesson.

4 If it's sunny, why do I feel cold.

5 You're a Gemini, aren't you.

The exclamation mark (!)

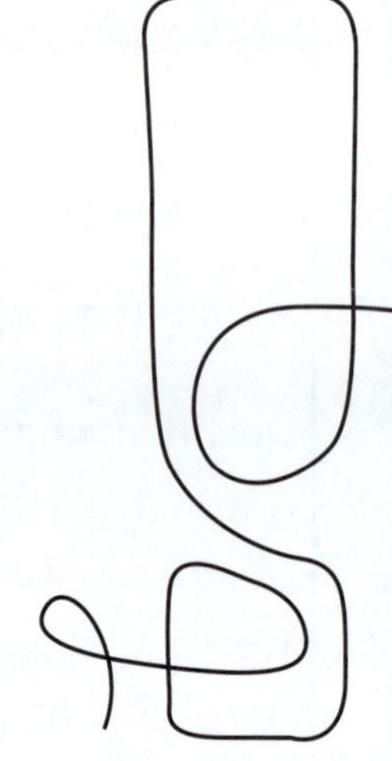

The exclamation mark is placed at the end of an order, an exclamation with strong emotion, or when somebody is shouting.

For example:

- Don't do that!
- Ask me first!
- Go away!
- No, I won't!
- Come here!

Because the exclamation mark behaves just like a full stop when it forms the end of the sentence, you do not need a full stop as well. Look carefully and you will see the exclamation mark includes a full stop: ! Remember: the next sentence must start with a capital letter.

YOUR TURN

These sentences need exclamation and/or question marks. Put them in.

1 I am ready. Let's go right now.

2 Are we there yet. I can't wait to get there.

3 Will Joanie be there when we arrive.

4 We've been driving for hours and hours. Will we ever get there.

5 Look, there's the bach. We're here at last.

The comma (,)

A comma is used to show a pause in a sentence.

For example: When he goes to the cricket nets, Adrian practises both bowling and batting.

A comma separates items in a list.

For example: The most common fruits include apples, pears, feijoas, kiwifruit and bananas.

Test to see if you need a comma. Read the sentence out loud and if you take a small breath, then that's where you put a comma.

YOUR TURN

Add commas to these sentences to make them easier to read.

1 My sister who usually finishes all her dinner suddenly refused to eat broccoli.

2 'I'm going to do my homework' said Manu.

3 If you are afraid of the dark take a torch with you.

4 Sally spoke in a whisper 'Who's there? Show yourself.'

 ISBN: 9780170499286

See if you can find good places for four commas in this piece from the internet about eating ice cream.

5 The sweetness of ice cream often combined with flavours like chocolate vanilla caramel or fruits provides a satisfying taste experience.

Speech marks (' ... ' or " ... ")

Speech marks are also called **inverted commas** or **quotation marks**.

A Speech marks are used to show direct speech – the words spoken.

For example: 'Kia ora,' called Moana from across the road.

Remember, every new speaker's words start on a new line. For example:

'Kia ora,' called Moana from across the road.

'Hey, are you going to the club?' asked Jason.

Moana responded immediately, 'No, not a chance.'

B Inverted commas can show the title of a movie, or play or book, etc.

For example: 'How to Train Your Dragon' is my favourite movie just now.

However, this can also be shown by using italics if you are typing.

For example: *How to Train Your Dragon* is my favourite movie just now.

C Speech marks can show words quoted from what someone has said or words someone has written.

For example: The words 'Take care of our children. Take care of what they hear: take care of what they feel. For how the children grow, will be the shape of Aotearoa' are a quote from Dame Whina Cooper.

YOUR TURN

Add speech marks/inverted commas to these short passages.

1 The classroom was quiet as all the students focused on their writing.

Sir, sir, Thomas said suddenly, breaking the silence.

Mr Smith looked up from his book. What is it, Tom? he asked.

Look, there's a huge dog loose in the playground.

Where? Mr Smith asked as he turned towards the windows. What kind of dog?

2 My favourite book of all time has to be Under the Mountain. It's set on Rangitoto Island and there's a book called Rangitoto by Maria Gill that I've read too.

3 Titles like Finding Nemo, Toy Story, Moana and Frozen are often recommended for children to view. The Incredibles, Stuart Little and Charlie and the Chocolate Factory are also listed as good films for family movie nights.

The apostrophe (')

A The apostrophe is used to show a contraction – where one or more letters are missed out, contracting two words into one.

For example:
He **does not** want to go. He **doesn't** want to go.
She will never ride a horse again. **She'll** never ride a horse again.

I **could have** got up earlier. (Not 'I could of'.)
I **could've** got up earlier.

We **would have** been here first thing if the car **had not** failed to start. (Not 'We would of'.)
We **would've** been here first thing if the car **hadn't** failed to start.

B The apostrophe is used to show possession with an s ('s).

For example:
- the child**'s** uniform
- a book**'s** cover
- the cook**'s** favourite recipe

We can get confused when the 'owner' is a word ending in 's'. Write the word first (for example, James, bus), then add **'s** for ownership.

For example:
- James**'s** shoes are black.
- The bus**'s** seats are green.

TIP: If in doubt, leave it out. If you don't know why you are using an apostrophe, leave it out. Write the contracted word or words in full (cannot, I have), or the possession without the apostrophe (childrens coats). Too many misplaced apostrophes are more confusing for a reader than the occasional missing one.

YOUR TURN

Each sentence needs two apostrophes. Add them.

1 Hengs favourite subject is biology because hes really interested in plants.

2 It mightve been cool outside today but the suns heat helped make the house warm.

3 Its hard to ride safely when my bikes lost its brakes.

4 Manu cant find his scooter because Toms taken it to his house.

5 You cannot trust Smithy. Hes a wolf in sheeps clothing.

There's a lot more to learn about punctuation, but for now these are the basics. If you can understand when and how to use these, you are well on your way to achieving the Literacy Writing assessment.

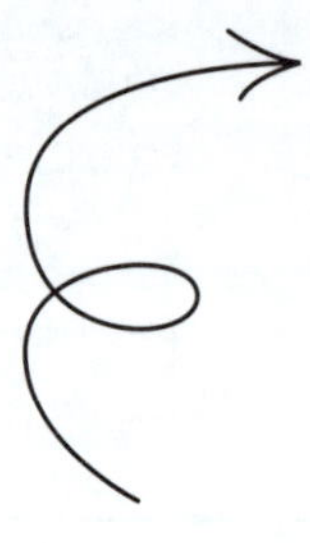

ISBN: 9780170499286

Spelling

Homophones

English does have a lot of words that sound the same but are spelled differently for different meanings. These are called homophones.

He can't **hear** me. Even though I'm right **here**.

Where will you **wear** that new hat?

The boat **creaked** as it floated down the **creek**.

The king, holding the **reins** of his horse, said, 'I **reign**. I am the king!'

She **knew** her friend's jacket was a **new** one.

YOUR TURN

1 In this sentence, would you use **would** or **wood**?

I'm building a table out of ________________.

2 How about this one – **piece** or **peace**?

The protest was in support of ________________.

A good way to practise using the correct version is to write one sentence using both words to show you know the meaning of each one. Choose the right word from the brackets to complete each sentence.

3 You will ______________ a letter to your koro ______________ now. (*write, right, rite*)

4 When is it ______________ birthday? If ______________ having a party, may I come? (*you're, your*)

5 Since last ______________ I've been drinking ______________ tea. (*weak, week*)

6 The girl ______________ she needed a ______________ pair of shoes. (*new, knew*)

7 The ______________ car had lots of ______________ in a box on the back seat. (*stationery/stationary*)

ISBN: 9780170499286

8 I read a __________ about a mermaid with a fish's __________. (*tail/tale*)

9 The student wrote a ______________ about ______________ for the magazine. (*piece/peace*)

10 The ______________ is sunny, but I can't decide ______________ to go outside or not. (*whether/weather*)

The only way to get this correct is to know the meaning and spelling of both words. One of the very best ways to learn the meaning and spelling of words is to read a lot.

Hint: How to choose the best answer

On the next 15 pages there are sets of practice questions to check that you are writing accurately. They are designed to be similar to the ones you will be asked in the Literacy Writing assessment.

Many of these questions will ask you to choose from four possible answers. These are called multi-choice questions. One excellent way to check that you have chosen the correct answer is to eliminate all the incorrect ones.

For example:

Select the option that uses the correction punctuation and capital letters.

Ⓐ the boy stood on the burning deck. — No. It does not have a capital letter at the beginning.

Ⓑ The boy stood, on the burning deck. — No. It has a comma where there is no pause.

Ⓒ The boy stood on the burning deck — No. It has no full stop.

Ⓓ ✓ The boy stood on the burning deck. — Yes. It's the only one left.

Now let's check your accuracy ...

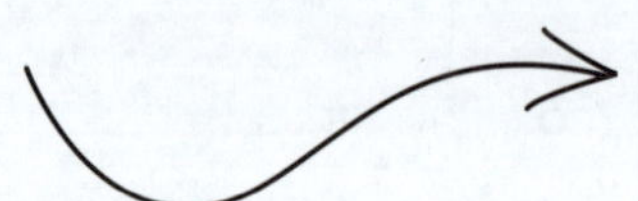

 ISBN: 9780170499286

Practice set 1

1 Select the correct word to finish the sentence accurately.

Hannah will _____ a green dress to the party.

- (A) wear
- (B) where
- (C) were
- (D) ware

2 Select the option that uses the correct punctuation and capital letters.

- (A) 'Are you coming to the play?' Asked Jane.
- (B) 'are you coming to the play?' asked Jane.
- (C) 'Are you coming to the play' asked Jane.
- (D) 'Are you coming to the play?' asked Jane.

3 Select the correct adjective to complete the sentence accurately.

This recipe tells you how to make the _____ cake I have ever baked.

- (A) tasty
- (B) most tastiest
- (C) tastiest
- (D) more tasty

4 Choose the word to complete the sentence accurately.

Kiera ______ go to the movies tonight because she has netball practice.

- (A) carnt
- (B) cant
- (C) can't
- (D) carn't

5 Select the correctly spelled word to finish the sentence accurately.

Tilly ______ a gift from her aunt in Timaru.

- (A) recieved
- (B) receeved
- (C) resieved
- (D) received

6 Select the correct formal words to replace the informal words in bold.

'Will you finish your homework tonight?'
'No worries.'

- (A) Yes, I will.
- (B) I'm not worried.
- (C) No, I'm worried.
- (D) Not likely.

7 Circle the best option in each shaded box to complete this sentence accurately.

It's | Its *clear that the* dogs | dog's *bone was buried in the* children's | childrens *sandpit.*

8 Select the option that uses the correct punctuation and capital letters.

- (A) on monday, we visited the auckland museum to research our history assignment.
- (B) On Monday we visited the Auckland Museum, to research our history assignment.
- (C) On Monday, we visited the Auckland Museum to research our history assignment.
- (D) On monday, we visited the Auckland museum to research our history assignment.

ISBN: 9780170499286

Practice set 2

1 Select the correct adjective to complete the sentence accurately.

In the cricket team, Rajiv is a _______ batsman than Aaron.

(A) more skilful
(B) skilful
(C) most skilful
(D) skilfuller

2 Select the correct pronoun to finish the sentence accurately.

The whole family ate ____ dinner at the table.

(A) there
(B) their
(C) they're
(D) thier

3 Which full stop and capital letter creates two accurate sentences?

Our local skatepark has ramps for beginners and experienced skaters it also has street skating equipment and concrete bowls.

(A) beginners. And
(B) skaters. It
(C) skating. Equipment
(D) equipment. And

4 Select the correct word to finish the sentence accurately.

'________ going to the party tomorrow?' asked Jonah.

(A) Whose
(B) Whos'e
(C) Who'se
(D) Who's

5 Replace the pronoun '**We**' with the correct words to explain who is watching a movie.

***We** are watching a movie.*

(A) Hone and me
(B) Me and Hone
(C) Hone and I
(D) I and Hone

6 Select the correct formal word or words to replace the informal word in bold.

*'**Chur** for helping me out!'*

(A) Charming
(B) Thankyou
(C) Ta heaps
(D) Thank you

7 Select the option that uses the correct punctuation.

(A) I prefer video games that are creative not destructive
(B) i prefer video games that are creative not destructive.
(C) I prefer video games that are creative, not destructive.
(D) I prefer video games, that are creative not destructive

8 Circle the best option in each shaded box to complete this sentence accurately.

My handwriting isn't very well | good *but I draw* well | good.

ISBN: 9780170499286

Practice set 3

1 Select the correctly spelled word to finish the sentence accurately.

We are going to the beach __________.

- (A) tomorow
- (B) tommorow
- (C) toomorrow
- (D) tomorrow

2 Select the option that uses the correct punctuation.

- (A) I packed my laptop my books my charger and a pen.
- (B) I packed my laptop, my books, my charger and a pen
- (C) I packed my laptop, my books, my charger and a pen.
- (D) i packed my laptop my books, my charger and a pen.

3 Select the correct adverb to complete the sentence accurately.

In the choir, Toby sings __________ than anyone else.

- (A) loud
- (B) loudly
- (C) more loudly
- (D) most loudly

4 Select the correct word to complete the sentence accurately.

All five trampers picked up _______ packs and set off into the bush.

- (A) there
- (B) their
- (C) thier
- (D) they're

5 Select the correct formal word to replace the informal word in bold.

'The train was ***chocka*** *this morning.'*

- (A) broken
- (B) choked
- (C) empty
- (D) full

6 Select the correct word to finish the sentence accurately.

Jade __________ accept Manu's invitation because she had to work that night.

- (A) couldn't
- (B) could'nt
- (C) cudn't
- (D) coul'dnt

7 Select the option that uses the correct punctuation.

- (A) The coach shouted hurry up were going to be late
- (B) The coach shouted, 'Hurry up! We're going to be late!'
- (C) the coach shouted 'hurry up! we're going to be late'
- (D) 'The coach shouted, hurry up, we're going to be late!'

8 Circle the best option in each shaded box to complete this sentence accurately.

I could barely hear | here *anything over the music, it was chaos for the* whole | hole *lunch break!*

ISBN: 9780170499286

Practice set 4

1 Select the option that uses the correct punctuation.

(A) 'Get up right NOW! Yelled Dad
(B) Get up right NOW! yelled Dad'
(C) 'Get up right NOW! Yelled Dad.
(D) 'Get up right NOW!' yelled Dad.

2 Select the correct word to finish the sentence accurately.

I ________ that hungry. One hamburger would have been enough.

(A) wasnt'
(B) was'nt
(C) wasnt
(D) wasn't

3 Select the correct word to finish the sentence accurately.

My sister is joining the army to be a ________.

(A) solider
(B) soldeir
(C) soldier
(D) solger

4 Select the correct pronoun to complete the sentence accurately.

'Wear ____ best shirt for the interview,' Mum advised.

(A) you're
(B) yours
(C) your
(D) youre

5 Select the correct adjective to complete the sentence accurately.

Simone is the _____ maths student in all of our class.

(A) good
(B) best
(C) better
(D) bestest

6 Circle the best option in the shaded box to complete this sentence accurately.

'Sleep well,' said | asked *the parent to the child.*

7 Select the option that uses the correct punctuation.

(A) every tuesday after school, jordan trains with the north harbour netball team
(B) Every Tuesday, after school Jordan trains with the North Harbour netball team.
(C) Every tuesday after school, Jordan trains with the North Harbour Netball team.
(D) Every Tuesday after school, Jordan trains with the North Harbour netball team.

8 Select the correct formal words to replace the informal words in bold.

*'I'll **give you a shout** when I get home.'*

(A) yell out
(B) call out to you
(C) be in touch
(D) buy you a drink

ISBN: 9780170499286

Practice set 5

1 Select the best place to put a comma in this sentence.

Install fire alarms in every bedroom living area and hallway in your house.

(A) alarms, in
(B) bedroom, living
(C) hallway, in
(D) living, area

2 Circle the best option in the shaded box to complete this sentence accurately.

The teacher seperated | separated *the two boys who were fighting.*

3 Select the option that uses the correct punctuation and capital letters.

(A) 'Loyal' by dave dobbyn has been voted NZs favourite song do you agree?
(B) 'Loyal' by Dave Dobbyn has been voted NZ's favourite Song. do you agree.
(C) 'Loyal' by Dave Dobbyn, has been Voted NZ's favourite song. Do you agree?
(D) 'Loyal' by Dave Dobbyn has been voted NZ's favourite song. Do you agree?

4 Select the correct pronoun to complete the sentence accurately.

I'm having breakfast with ___ aunty tomorrow.

(A) my
(B) mine
(C) me
(D) myself

5 Select the correct adverb to complete the sentence accurately.

The audience at the theatre applauded ______________.

(A) cheerful
(B) cheerfully
(C) most cheerful
(D) more cheerful

6 Select the correct word to finish the sentence accurately.

Greta wants to go to ____ house tomorrow.

(A) you're
(B) yours
(C) yore
(D) your

7 Select the correct formal words to replace the informal words in bold.

We're moving out of town ***into the wops*** *next year.*

(A) to a different place
(B) to a place called Wops
(C) to a more rural area
(D) to a place far away

8 Select the option that uses the correct punctuation.

(A) Is the movie *Dog Man* worth watching
(B) Is the movie dog man worth watching?
(C) is the movie *Dog Man* worth watching?
(D) Is the movie *Dog Man* worth watching?

ISBN: 9780170499286

Practice set 6

1 Select the correctly spelled word to finish the sentence accurately.

This is ___________ the correct answer.

(A) definitely
(B) definitly
(C) defiantly
(D) definately

2 Select the correct form of pronoun to complete the sentence accurately.

This backpack belongs to Sophie. It is _____.

(A) her
(B) hers'
(C) hers
(D) her's

3 Select the correct adjective to complete the sentence accurately.

'That pie was the ____ I've ever tasted,' complained Jack.

(A) baddest
(B) worse
(C) worst
(D) worstest

4 Where is the best place for a full stop to turn one sentence into two?

(A) I'll be at school tomorrow I'll be early and. I'll bring my guitar.
(B) I'll be at school tomorrow. I'll be early and I'll bring my guitar.
(C) I'll be at school tomorrow I'll be early. And I'll bring my guitar.
(D) I'll be at school. Tomorrow I'll be early and I'll bring my guitar.

5 Select the best place to put a comma in this sentence.

When storing a sleeping bag it is better to roll it up rather than fold it.

(A) storing, a
(B) bag, it
(C) up, rather
(D) than, fold

6 Select the correct words to finish the sentence accurately.

Did you ___ _________ in the flood?

(A) lose anythink
(B) loose anything
(C) lose anything
(D) loose anythink

7 Select the correct words to finish the sentence accurately.

It's _____ use waiting any longer because the bus won't come _____.

(A) know, no
(B) no, now
(C) know, now
(D) no, know

8 Select the option that uses the correct punctuation.

(A) In the North Island a holiday home is called a 'bach'. In the South Island it is often called a 'crib'.
(B) In the North Island a holiday home is called a bach. In the South Island it is often called a 'crib'.
(C) In the North Island a holiday home is called a 'bach' in the South Island it is often called a 'crib'
(D) In the north island a holiday home is called a 'bach'. In the south island it is often called a 'crib'.

ISBN: 9780170499286

Practice set 7

1 Select the correct pronoun to complete the sentence accurately.

'____ lot shouldn't be here, ______ trespassing!' yelled the security guard.

(A) You, you're
(B) Yous, your
(C) Youse you're
(D) You, your

2 Select the correct word to finish the sentence accurately.

I _________ taken the bus home after school.

(A) should
(B) should've
(C) should of
(D) shud've

3 Select the correct adverbs to complete the sentence accurately.

Kevin plays tennis ___________ but Karl plays __________ than him.

(A) good, gooder
(B) well, weller
(C) well, better
(D) good, better

4 Select the correctly spelled word to finish the sentence accurately.

Aroha used a pair of ________ to cut her doll's hair.

(A) sissors
(B) scissors
(C) scisors
(D) sizzors

5 Select the option that uses capital letters correctly.

(A) The White Ferns are playing in wellington next week.
(B) The White ferns are playing in Wellington next week.
(C) The white Ferns are playing in wellington next week.
(D) The White Ferns are playing in Wellington next week.

6 Circle the best option in each shaded box to complete this sentence accurately.

I brought | bought *my laptop to class,* but | because *I forgot to charge it.*

7 Select the option that uses the correct punctuation.

(A) At the barbecue I said, 'Let's eat Tommy.'
(B) At the barbecue I said, 'Let's eat, Tommy.'

8 Circle the best option in the shaded box to complete this sentence accurately.

My aunt will come to stay with us tomorrow | yesterday.

ISBN: 9780170499286

Practice set 8

1 Select the correct words for this sentence.

There is too ______ sugar in my tea and too ___ biscuits on my plate.

(A) much, much
(B) many, many
(C) much, many
(D) many, much

2 Select the option that uses the correct words and punctuation.

(A) me and my sister were born on the same day. We're twins.
(B) Me and my sister were born on the same day. We're twins.
(C) My sister and me were born on the same day. We're twins.
(D) My sister and I were born on the same day. We're twins.

3 Replace the pronoun **us** to show who is being watched.

The science teacher watched ***us*** *complete the experiment safely.*

(A) he and Tim
(B) Tim and him
(C) Tim and me
(D) me and Tim

4 Select the correctly spelled word to finish the sentence accurately.

The boy ____ his lunch to school.

(A) brought
(B) bought
(C) bringed
(D) brung

5 Select the correct word to finish the sentence accurately.

Do you know when it's your ________ birthday?

(A) mothers
(B) mother's
(C) mothers'
(D) mothers's

6 Select the correct word to finish the sentence accurately.

Eva chose an egg _______ for her lunch.

(A) sandwich
(B) sandwhich
(C) sandwitch
(D) sanwich

7 Select the option that uses capital letters accurately.

(A) *Rangers Apprentice* is a series of novels written by australian author John Flanagan.
(B) *Ranger's apprentice* is a series of novels written by australian author john Flanagan.
(C) *Ranger's Apprentice* is a series of novels written by Australian author John Flanagan.
(D) *ranger's apprentice* is a series of novels written by Australian author john flanagan.

8 Circle the best option in each shaded box to complete these sentences accurately.

Two | Too | To *noisy children ran through the supermarket. Their mum asked them* two | too | to *calm down.*

ISBN: 9780170499286

Practice set 9

1 Select the option that uses the correct punctuation.

(A) Do you think you'll be able to eat all that food?' asked Dad.

(B) 'Do you think you'll be able to eat all that food? asked Dad.

(C) 'Do you think you'll be able to eat all that food?' asked Dad.

(D) Do you think you'll be able to eat all that food? asked Dad.

2 Select the correctly spelled word to finish the sentence accurately.

The library is usually a very ______ place.

(A) quite

(B) queit

(C) cwiet

(D) quiet

3 Select the correct verbs to complete the sentence accurately.

When the bell ________, the class ________ work immediately.

(A) rings, stopped

(B) rang, stops

(C) rang, stopped

(D) rings, stopping

4 Replace the **nouns** in bold with the appropriate pronouns.

*Samoan is Edward's second language and **Edward** speaks **Samoan** really well.*

(A) he, it

(B) him, that

(C) his, it

(D) he's, that

5 Circle the best option in each shaded box to complete the sentence accurately.

George is taller | tallest | more tall *than William but William is* better | good | best *at basketball.*

6 Select the correctly spelled word to finish the sentence accurately.

Our tramping group found the ____________ very comfortable.

(A) accommodation

(B) acomodation

(C) accomodation

(D) accomadation

7 Circle the best option in each shaded box to complete this sentence accurately.

We saw a huge whale swimming in the see | sea. Its | It's *tail was enormous.*

8 Which punctuation mark completes this sentence accurately?

'I'll meet you at the park later, okay__

(A) .

(B) '?

(C) ?

(D) ?'

Practice set 10

1 Select the correctly spelled word to finish the sentence accurately.

New Zealand was the first country in the world where _______ had the right to vote.

- (A) wimmin
- (B) woman
- (C) wommen
- (D) women

2 Select the option that completes the sentence accurately.

Video games use an input device such as a ...

- (A) joystick controller, keyboard or motion sensing device.
- (B) joystick, controller keyboard or motion sensing device.
- (C) joystick, controller, keyboard or motion sensing device.
- (D) joystick, controller, keyboard or, motion sensing device.

3 Select the correctly spelled word to finish the sentence accurately.

The ______ is where I find lots of good books.

- (A) libray
- (B) libery
- (C) library
- (D) liberary

4 Which words in this sentence need capital letters?

cycle alongside the grey river to its mouth before turning and following the dramatic tasman sea coastline to paroa.

- (A) Grey, Tasman, Sea, Coastline, Paroa
- (B) Cycle, Grey, River, Tasman, Sea, Paroa
- (C) Cycle, Grey, River, Paroa
- (D) Grey, River, Tasman, Sea, Paroa

5 Select the correct verb tense to complete the sentence accurately.

At the moment Principal Adams ______ in assembly.

- (A) speaks
- (B) was speaking
- (C) is speaking
- (D) spoke

6 Circle the best option in each shaded box to complete this sentence accurately.

Were | Where | We're *meeting up after school, but no one said exactly* were | where | we're *we should go.*

7 Choose the correct pronoun to complete the sentence accurately.

Moana and Alexa are sisters who share a bedroom. It is ______.

- (A) their
- (B) theirs'
- (C) their's
- (D) theirs

8 Select the option that uses the correct punctuation.

- (A) Im going to join the volleyball team.
- (B) I'm going to join the Volleyball team
- (C) I'm going to join the volleyball team.
- (D) Im going to join the Volleyball team.

ISBN: 9780170499286

Practice set 11

1 Select the correct verb to complete the sentence accurately.

Keri ___ ______ several pairs of glasses online.

(A) has buyed
(B) has brunged
(C) has bought
(D) has brought

2 Select the option that uses the correct punctuation.

(A) I speak te reo maori.
(B) I speak Te Reo Māori?
(C) I speak te reo Māori.
(D) I speak te reo Maorī.

3 Select the correctly spelled word to finish the sentence accurately.

Maisie has to _______ a letter to her aunt in Australia.

(A) right
(B) wright
(C) rite
(D) write

4 Circle the best option in the shaded box to complete this sentence accurately.

We stayed at school late because | although *we had a football game after class.*

5 Select the option that uses the correct punctuation.

(A) Im serious, I am not going to eat Marmite ever!
(B) I'm serious, I am not going to eat Marmite ever!
(C) I'm serious I am not, going to eat Marmite ever.
(D) Im serious I am not going to eat Marmite ever

6 Select the correct use of capital letters to complete the sentence accurately.

six kiwi were released into the nz bush last tuesday night.

(A) Six, Nz
(B) Six, Kiwi, NZ, Tuesday
(C) Six, NZ, Tuesday
(D) Six, NZ

7 Select the correct pronouns to complete the sentence accurately.

'If _____ going to the mall, please buy a new pen for ___ sister,' said Mum.

(A) your, your
(B) you're, you're
(C) you're, your
(D) your, yours

8 Select the correctly spelled word to finish the sentence accurately.

Joe blushed with __________ when he was speaking in assembly.

(A) embarasment
(B) embarrassment
(C) embarassment
(D) embarassedment

Practice set 12

1 Which full stop and capital letter creates two accurate sentences?

Jake's having dinner at Sefina's place tonight he's hoping to have curry.

(A) Sefina's. Place
(B) hoping. To
(C) tonight. He's
(D) dinner. At

2 Select the correct words to complete the sentence accurately.

___ time for our car to have ___ engine checked.

(A) it's its
(B) It's, its
(C) Its, it's
(D) Its, its

3 Select the correct verb to complete the sentence accurately.

When I shopped online, there ___ no problems with delivery.

(A) was
(B) were
(C) wasn't
(D) weren't

4 Select the correct formal word or words to replace the informal word in bold.

'I've got ***heaps*** *of bike parts in the garage,' claimed Simon.*

(A) a lot
(B) many
(C) some
(D) a few

5 Select the option that uses the correct punctuation and capital letters.

(A) during social studies, emily and i worked on a slideshow about the treaty of waitangi.
(B) During Social Studies, Emily and I worked on a slideshow about the Treaty of Waitangi.
(C) During Social Studies Emily and I worked on a slideshow about the treaty of Waitangi.
(D) During social studies, Emily and I worked on a slideshow about the treaty of waitangi.

6 Select the correctly spelled word to complete the sentence accurately.

Today is ________. It is your birthday.

(A) speshal
(B) speciul
(C) speshul
(D) special

7 Which sentence uses commas correctly?

(A) Hana lives on, pasta, cheese jam and peanut butter.
(B) Hana lives on pasta, cheese, jam and peanut butter.
(C) Hana lives on pasta cheese, jam and peanut butter.
(D) Hana lives on pasta, cheese jam and peanut butter.

8 Circle the best option in each shaded box to complete this sentence accurately.

She is a quiet | quite *person and she paints* beautiful | beautifully.

ISBN: 9780170499286

Practice set 13

1 Select the correctly spelled words to complete the sentence accurately.

I asked for ___ donuts when I went ___ the bakery.

- (A) to, to
- (B) too, to
- (C) two, to
- (D) two, too

2 Select the option that uses the correct punctuation.

- (A) Mia packed snacks a speaker a blanket and her phone.
- (B) Mia packed snacks, a speaker a blanket and her phone
- (C) Mia packed, snacks, a speaker, a blanket and her phone.
- (D) Mia packed snacks, a speaker, a blanket and her phone.

3 Circle the best option in the shaded box to complete this sentence accurately.

He missed the bus, so | because | but *he had to walk to school.*

4 Select the correctly spelled word to complete the sentence accurately.

We must care for our ________.

- (A) environment
- (B) enviroment
- (C) invironment
- (D) envirenment

5 Select the correct pronouns to complete the sentence accurately.

'If __ can't go, then ___ can't either,' I said to my brother.

- (A) I, you
- (B) me, you
- (C) I, youse
- (D) I, your

6 Select the correct verbs to complete the sentence accurately.

When Joe _____ his homework, he _____ outside to play.

- (A) finish, go
- (B) finished, goes
- (C) finished, went
- (D) finishes, went

7 Select the correct formal word to replace the informal word in bold.

'The surfing here is ***sweet****!' exclaimed Aroha.*

- (A) awful
- (B) useless
- (C) excellent
- (D) okay

8 Select the option that uses the correct punctuation for an instruction.

- (A) 'Give me a call when you know what time the game is on?'
- (B) 'give me a call when you know what time the game is on'.
- (C) 'Give me a call when you know what time the game is on.'
- (D) Give me a call when you know what time the game is on'

ISBN: 9780170499286

Practice set 14

1 Select the correct words to complete the sentence accurately.

_____ bikes are the red ones, over _____.

- (A) They're, their
- (B) They're, their
- (C) There, there
- (D) Their, there

2 Circle the best option in the shaded box to complete this sentence accurately.

You can work with a partner and | unless *you'd rather do it on your own.*

3 Select the correct words to finish the sentences accurately.

____ cycle to the old ____ this afternoon. ____ you come too?

- (A) we'll, well, will
- (B) Wheel, well, Wil
- (C) Well, well, will
- (D) We'll, well, Will

4 Select the correct verb to complete the sentence accurately.

When Maie turns sixteen, she ________ to Rarotonga by herself to visit her grandma.

- (A) gone
- (B) going
- (C) will go
- (D) has gone

5 Select the correct formal words to replace the informal words in bold.

'Sorry I'm late. I missed the bus.'
*'**Sweet as**, we're not busy yet.'*

- (A) That's cool
- (B) That's not a problem
- (C) That's nice
- (D) That's all good

6 Select the correctly spelled word to complete the sentence accurately.

The netball team plays on the hard _____ outside in winter.

- (A) cort
- (B) caught
- (C) court
- (D) caout

7 Select the option that completes the sentence accurately.

A pūkana helps to emphasise a point in a song or haka and ...

- (A) demonstrate the performer's ferocity intensity or passion
- (B) demonstrate the performers ferocity, intensity or passion.
- (C) demonstrate the performers ferocity, intensity or passion
- (D) demonstrate the performer's ferocity, intensity or passion.

8 Select the option that uses commas to complete the sentence accurately.

A dairy is a shop licensed to sell groceries, ...

- (A) eggs milk dairy products perishables, newspapers and other goods.
- (B) eggs, milk, dairy products, perishables, newspapers and other goods.
- (C) eggs, milk, dairy products perishables newspapers and other goods.
- (D) eggs, milk dairy products, perishables, newspapers and other goods

ISBN: 9780170499286

Practice set 15

1 Select the option that uses the correct punctuation.

(A) 'Which class is going swimming today'? asked the teacher.
(B) Which class is going swimming today?' asked the teacher.
(C) 'Which class is going swimming today? asked the teacher
(D) 'Which class is going swimming today?' asked the teacher.

2 Select the correct formal words to replace the informal words in bold.

'Thanks for giving me a lift.'
*'**All good**.'*

(A) You're welcome
(B) No problemo
(C) Totally excellent
(D) No worries

3 Select the correct words to finish the sentences accurately.

____ dirty dishes are those? ____ doing the washing-up tonight?

(A) Whose, Who's
(B) Who's, Who's
(C) Who's, Whose
(D) Whose, Whose

4 Select the correct verb to complete the sentence accurately.

'Have you seen Liam?'
'Yes, I ___ him yesterday.'

(A) see
(B) saw
(C) seem
(D) see'd

5 Select the correct pronouns to complete the sentence accurately.

Please give the tickets to _____ so we can enter the game by _______.

(A) us, ourself
(B) us, ourselves
(C) us, ourselfs
(D) we, ourselves

6 Select the correctly written words to complete the sentence accurately.

There is an island in New Zealand called _____ ______.

(A) Grate Barrier
(B) great barrier
(C) Great Barrier
(D) Great barrier

7 Circle the best option in the shaded box to complete this sentence accurately.

My favourite part of a meal is
dessert | desert.

8 Select the correct word to complete the sentence accurately.

Sami had finished her homework ________ by 8 pm.

(A) completely
(B) completly
(C) compleetly
(D) completley

ISBN: 9780170499286

Let's get writing

Kia tuhi tātou

In the Literacy Writing assessment you will be directed to write **TWO pieces** of different text types and lengths.

You will be marked on:

- **length:** writing a minimum of 150 words or 250 words depending on the prompt
- **ideas:** providing information and details that are appropriate for your audience and purpose

- **structure:** organising your ideas clearly and appropriately, with a clear beginning, middle and ending
- **language choices:** choosing words and sentences that are appropriate for your audience and purpose
- **accuracy:** using correct spelling, punctuation and grammar.

This workbook will:

- **give you a place to write a plan.** Some students go off the topic when they start writing. By writing a plan you will improve the content of your writing.
- **guide you on how to structure your writing.** Some students forget to use paragraphs when they are writing in a test. By the time you have completed all the work in this book, you will never make that mistake.
- **offer advice** about the vocabulary you choose to use.
- **build your confidence.** As you use the advice in this book, you will develop your own writing skills. You will learn to approach any writing task, including those in the Literacy Writing assessment, with confidence.

Let's get started ...

ISBN: 9780170499286

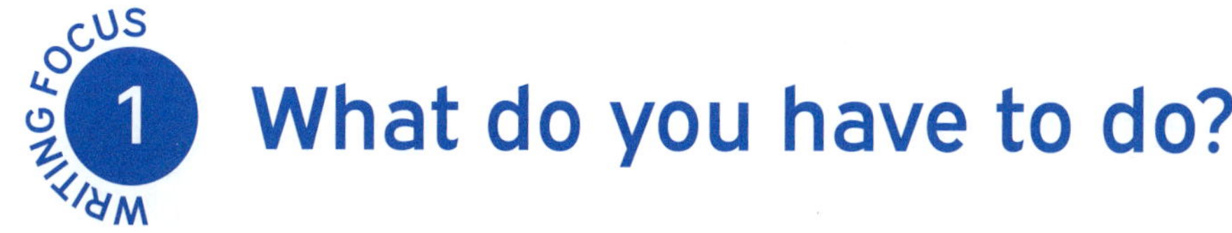

What do you have to do?

The Literacy Writing assessment requires you to write two pieces in formal accurate English. You must read each question carefully and follow the instructions. This seems simple but often students feel hurried and don't do what the assessment tells them to do.

If you understand what you have to do before you begin writing:

- you show that you have understood what you have read
- you show that you can follow instructions
- you will complete the assessment with confidence.

How might this part of an assessment go wrong?
• *Student skim reads the topic too quickly and misses important instructions.*
• *Student forgets who they are writing to.*
• *Student goes off topic quickly.*
• *Student writes too few words (or too many).*

Let's look at a strategy for understanding the question

We want you to follow a clear process to make sure you are reading a question thoroughly. Then you will not miss anything important. For each question, stop and look at it carefully to make sure you fully understand what you are being asked to do.

Follow these steps:

1. Read the whole question – **twice**.
2. Check any words in **bold**. They must be important.
3. Circle/highlight the actual **topic** you must write about.
4. Circle/highlight the **type of text** you are writing and note what this requires. Is it a blog? An article? An email?
5. Circle/highlight any **names** or **specific details** you have been given.
6. Circle/highlight anything you might need to **invent**.
7. Check **how many words** you must write. More words need more ideas.
8. Read all the **prompts** or extra information you are given. Use them.
9. Be sure you know **who** you are writing to, and **why** (Audience and Purpose).
10. **Reread** the question to confirm you haven't missed anything.

ISBN: 9780170499286

Taking a closer look at a question

Let's see how one student used the 10-step process to make sure she knew exactly what she was being asked to do. Before writing anything, she highlighted all the most important details by going through those steps. Look at her annotations and link them to the steps on the previous page.

4 Dear/Yours sincerely

QUESTION: Formal letter

Your school is starting a work experience programme for senior students. 5

9 3

Write a letter to a local business (real or imagined) in your area (e.g. a café, mechanic, hair salon, vet, office) asking if they would be interested in hosting a student for a short work placement. 5

6 hairdresser

Write between 150 and 250 words.

7

You might like to write about:

- Introducing the idea.
- Why that type of business is of interest.
- What students could do at that business.
- How long would the work experience be?
- How would it help the student and the business?
- Thanking them and asking for a reply.

8 Maybe hairdresser, assist stylist, one day, suitability to this job, possible employee ...

We'll circle back to this question later.

This process reminded her to:

- write **a letter** that needs a formal layout at the start and the end
- write to a **local business person**, Ms Smith if all else fails!
- **ask for a favour**, a placement for a senior student
- write at least **150 words**
- use the **prompts**.

Taking two minutes to **explore the question properly** and to **think before you write** is a really good way to ensure that you stay on topic and actually answer the question.

This preparation will help you to pass the Literacy Writing assessment with ease.

Now let's compare two students' work to see how following this process helps.

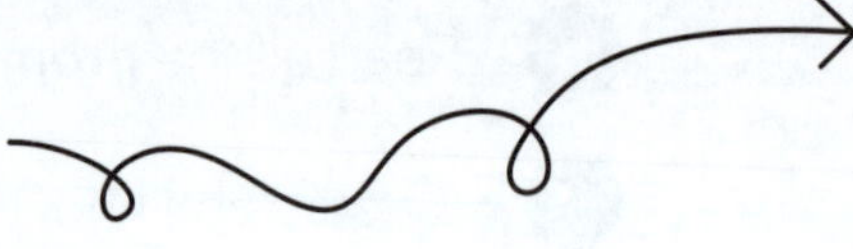

 ISBN: 9780170499286

Seeing is believing ...

Two students answer the same question. One of them follows all the steps of the process. One does not.

STUDENT 1

QUESTION: Article

Everyone in your class has been asked to write an article for the school newspaper.

Your topic is: **Why exercise is good for teenagers.**

get fit

Write between 150 and 250 words.

In your answer, you could:

- identify different kinds of fitness
- describe the ways fitness brings benefits
- give reasons why fitness is important.

outdoors

not computers

Now read Student 1's answer.

No heading

Who's the audience? Can you tell this is for a newspaper?

Is it long enough? No, it's only 125 words.

I think exercise is a good thing for teenagers. Teenagers often don't get outside much because they spend a lot of time on the computer playing games and this means they are not as fit as they could be.

Teenagers could get outside to get fit. They could play games on the field at lunchtime instead of being inside all the time on their computers or phones. They could also play in the gym at basketball or netball when it is raining.

Teenagers should get fit because it is good for them and they will feel the benefit when they get older. I think teenagers should try to get fit and keep fit and not sit about inside on the computer all day and night.

Is it on topic? It does talk about teenagers. It does mention some sports. But it talks about playing on computers as much as it does about exercise.

It's a bit vague about why being fit is a good thing.

Now let's look at how Student 2 used the process.

Let's take a look at Student 2's annotation for the same question.

text type = article

audience = school community, parents and students

STUDENT 2

QUESTION: Article

Everyone in your class has been asked to write an article for the school newspaper.

explain why fitness is important = feel good, success

Your topic is: **Why exercise is good for teenagers.**

topic = why = give reasons. Exercise = fitness/moving body, good = positives, teenagers = my age

Write between 150 and 250 words.

number of words max 250 = 5 paragraphs

In your answer, you could:

- identify different kinds of fitness
- describe the ways fitness brings benefits
- give reasons why fitness is important.

identify = running, swimming, games

describe the benefits = strength, heart, mental health

Can you see that this annotation helps the student understand their task more completely?

Now read Student 2's answer.

text type = article. Added a heading.

Exercise and Teenagers

Exercise should be an important part of daily life for teenagers. We need to keep our bodies and our minds healthy and exercise will help us do this.

para 1 mentions exercise and teenagers = topic is correct

clear structure (link to para beginnings)

Firstly, teenagers have many opportunities to get fit. They can take part in PE at school which could be in the school gym or playing sport on the fields. Swimming, running, biking or skateboarding are all ways teenagers can keep fit easily at home too.

identify = mentions several sports

Secondly, taking part in any physical exercise, like playing soccer or running or swimming, makes our muscles strong and keeps our bodies developing in a way that means we are fit. Exercise also makes our heart strong so we are healthy, too. Sitting in front of a computer cannot do that, so teenagers should spend time every day doing some exercise.

describe = muscles, growing, heart benefits

Thirdly, physical exercise makes us feel good and could lead to getting into sports teams. Also, teenagers who take part in exercise are going to feel better in themselves. Our mental health will be better than if we do not take part in some sort of exercise. Even just walking the dog is better than nothing.

explain = leads to success, and better mental health

In conclusion, exercise is good for teenagers because it helps our bodies and minds to be fit. Doing any sort of exercise every day will keep us healthier and happier.

220 words in 5 paragraphs = meets the word requirement

 ISBN: 9780170499286

Have a go ...

Now use the advice from page 71 to help you annotate a question on your own.

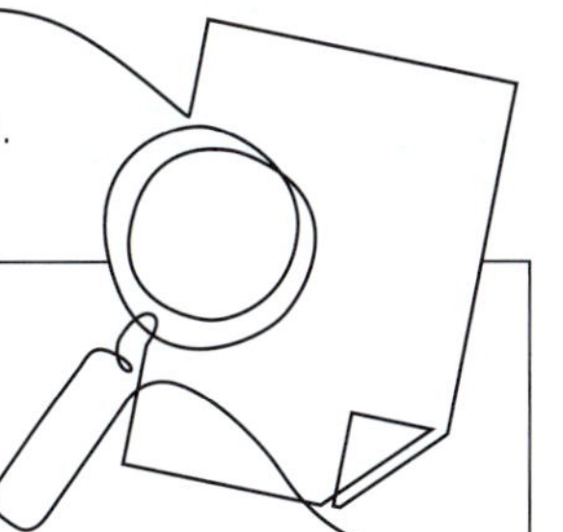

QUESTION: Email

Your local cycle path has not been repaired for two years. Write an email to your local Council Environmental Officer, Alan Mauga, explaining **what** is wrong and **why** you think it should be looked after more regularly.

Give your email the subject line: Waterview Cycle Path Needs Help

Write 150–250 words.

You might include:

- current problems for cyclists
- how the path used to be
- what you think should be done
- what benefits there would be to repairing the path.

So now that you are more confident using the question to help you prepare a great piece of writing, let's look at audience and purpose in more detail ...

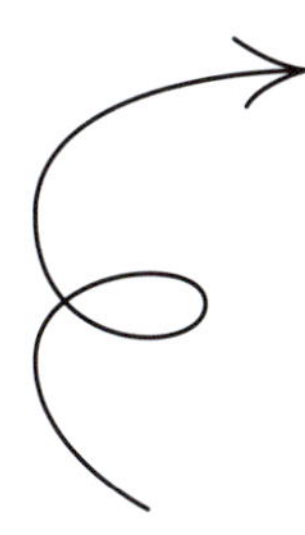

WRITING FOCUS 2

Who is your audience, what is your purpose?

The two words 'audience' and 'purpose' are mentioned in the Literacy Writing marking criteria. This means being aware of WHO you are writing for (audience) and WHY you are writing (purpose).

If you know your audience and your purpose, you will write in the appropriate tone. (Think ***tone of voice***.) If you are making a request, polite words such as 'please' and 'thank you' are important words to use. If you are criticising something, then formal negative words such as 'polluted' rather than 'yucky' are appropriate.

Our best advice is to keep your writing polite and formal.

How might this part of an assessment go wrong?

- *Student forgets **why** they are writing.*
- *Student forgets **who** will read their words.*
- *Student writes as if they are just thinking aloud.*

Audience is a bit tricky. Students often forget this part. After all, you do a lot of writing but mostly it is for your teacher.

The question will tell you who your audience is but sometimes this isn't explicit. Here are some examples to illustrate how the question implies the audience.

Question/topic	The audience is ...
Write an article for your local newspaper	your community, anyone who reads the local paper
Write an article for your school's newsletter, website, magazine	your school community, parents, caregivers, teachers, pupils, board of trustees
Write an article for your school's intranet	your fellow students, your teachers, senior leadership, board of trustees
Write an email to your Principal, Careers Adviser, Canteen Manager, etc.	someone you know who is an elder, a person in authority, you may know them
Write an email to a local person in charge of something, mayor, councillor, journalist, etc.	someone you do not know personally but who is in a position of responsibility
Write a letter to a friend	someone you know well
Write a letter to a relative	someone you may know well
Write a blog post	the whole world

ISBN: 9780170499286

Purpose is reasonably straightforward. You might be:

Persuading someone about something
- We should buy less food wrapped in plastic.
- Our local council should build a skatepark.
- The school canteen should open after school.

Explaining something
- Why exercise is good for us.
- How a teenager can save money.
- A person I admire is ...

Giving an **opinion**
- Why I like holidays.
- Why I think sport should be optional.
- Why computer games are good for teenagers.

Describing something
- A place I love.
- My favourite food.
- A memorable moment.

As far as the Literacy Writing assessment is concerned, just remember that whoever your audience is, keep it formal.

Write:
- **politely**
- **in a structured format**
- **in formal language**
- **accurately.**

Sometimes, layout is important ...

The question will tell you the type of text you need to write, and some text types have specific layout requirements. At this level, you don't need to include every detail, but using the basics can help you stay organised and on track. For example:

A letter is written to a person, so an opening salutation is necessary:

Dear Mr/Ms/Mrs plus their name
or
Dear Sir/Madam

A closing salutation is also required:

Yours sincerely/Kind regards

An email is written to a person, so an opening salutation is necessary:

To Mr/Ms/Mrs
or
Hello/Hi plus the name if the person is a friend or family
A brief closing salutation is also required: *Regards/Thank you*

An article, whether in print or online, will have a headline.
A blog will have a headline.

ISBN: 9780170499286

Have a go ...

Look at the following questions. Identify the purpose and audience for each.

QUESTION	PURPOSE	AUDIENCE
	Persuade; explain; describe; opinion	Community; fellow students; an elder; someone in authority; teacher; Board of Trustees; a stranger; the whole world
Write an article for your local paper called *Technology makes our lives easier.* Do you agree or disagree? Explain your answer with reasons and examples.		
Write a set of instructions for someone who is new to your favourite hobby or sport. This will be in a blog on your school intranet.		
Your local cafe, Oliver's, is advertising in the local newspaper for a school student to work clearing tables. Write a letter applying for the job.		
Some schools have a later start time for students. Do you think your school should start later? Explain your opinion in an email to your principal with reasons and examples.		
Write about a time you learned something important from a mistake for your end-of-year magazine.		

Let's take a closer look at the way the prompts can help ...

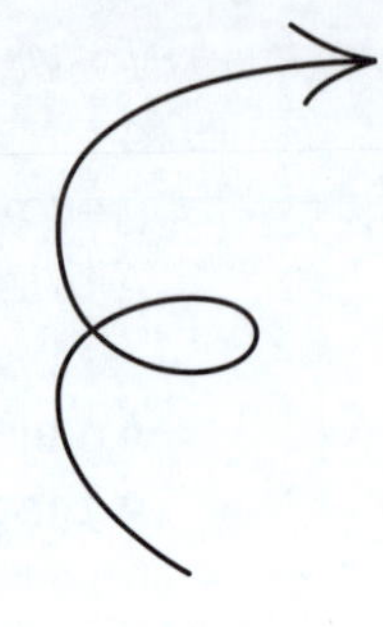

 ISBN: 9780170499286

Use the prompts to plan

To help you stay on task, the question will likely give you some prompts.
These may be written prompts or an image or a mix of both.
They are ideas about what to include in your writing.
This is what helps you PLAN your writing.

The prompts may **tell you** what to write about:

- You **should** include ...
- You **must** include ...

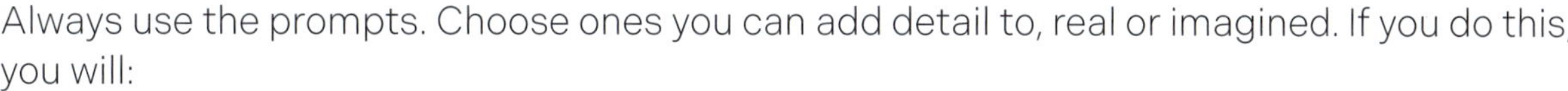

Or what you **could** write about:

- You **might** include ...
- **Possible ideas** are ...

Always use the prompts. Choose ones you can add detail to, real or imagined. If you do this, you will:

- make a plan quickly
- start writing knowing what you are going to say
- stay on topic for your whole text.

How might this part of an assessment go wrong?

- *Student spends too much time trying to think what to write without using the prompts and feels rushed.*
- *Student ignores prompts and goes off topic.*

Let's take a look at one question's prompts

Below is a question similar to those in the assessment. Pay careful attention to the provided prompts.

QUESTION: Blog
You have been asked to write a blog piece for your school's intranet.

Your topic is: **Part-time work for school students: is it good or bad?**

Write between 150 and 250 words.

In your answer, you **should** include:

- What part-time work means
- Examples of part-time work

In your answer, you **might** include:

- Earning money
- Failing at school
- Learning to be responsible
- Voluntary work
- Being stressed
- Confidence

Remember, you will be marked on: length, ideas, structure, language, audience, purpose, accuracy. See page 70 for more detail.

Here are the plans two students completed for this task.
Which plan will make the final writing easier?

STUDENT 1

- **Part-time** — not school time
- Supermarket, fast food
- **Money** for stuff
- **Responsibility** — get up
- **Stress** — too much time
- **Voluntary** — work not paid
- **Confidence**

STUDENT 2

- **Part-time** — after school, weekends, flexible jobs in shops and cafes
- **Money** — to help family, pay own way, helps me be independent
- **Responsibility** — have to turn up on time, deal with people, strangers
- **Stress** — might be issue with school work
- **Voluntary** work could be way to start
- **Confidence** — dealing with life beyond family and school

Hopefully you can see that Student 2 is going to write their answer much more easily than Student 1 because they have thought of a lot more ideas to use.

STUDENT 1'S BLOG PIECE

Restates the topic as the title.

Should teenagers have part-time jobs while they are at school?

Student has written 6 separate, mostly single sentence paragraphs following the prompts.

Teenagers should be able to have part-time work at the weekends. They could have a job after school too.

If they have a job and earn their own money, then they don't have to keep asking their family, their parents or other people in their family for cash.

If they have a job, a teenager has to get up to go to the job so they learn to be responsible for their time.

A job might be a problem if the student doesn't do their schoolwork though. Then they might get a bit stressed.

Ideas there, just not developed.

If they want, they can do volunteer work, like for example they may want to help look after an animal like a horse and get free rides in return.

Having a job can make a teenager more confident too.

143 words, so a bit short.

No conclusion.

ISBN: 9780170499286

STUDENT 2'S BLOG PIECE

A part-time job is good for school students and for their families

Has a heading made by bolding first sentence.

5 complete paragraphs. More than one sentence in all but the last one.

Part-time work has many benefits for school students. It can be after school, such as in the local shop or supermarket. It can be at weekends such as helping on a farm or in a hair salon. It can be working at flexible times by babysitting or delivering newspapers. Many students do some sort of part-time work, either paid or unpaid.

In the first place, if a student earns some money of their own, they don't have to rely on family for money all the time. Then they can buy their own snacks or drinks or personal things. This helps the family finances and means the student is more independent.

Secondly, a student who hasn't had to be responsible for much now has to get to the job on time and do the work well, which means they learn to be more responsible. For example, if you are serving in a shop, you have to smile and talk to the customers politely all the time, even if you don't feel like it.

Thirdly, students can get a lot of confidence from doing a part-time job well. They can then be more confident at school and might even learn what sort of work they want to do in life after school.

Finally, a part-time job for a teenager is a step on the way to being more independent of their family, more responsible and more confident in their life.

Use of sequencing words to start each paragraph.

The student has used some (not all) of their ideas and expanded with examples.

250 words – just right!

YOU DO:

Using two highlighters, go through the blog post above and highlight in the first colour every word the student uses from the prompts, and in the second colour every added detail the student gives to those prompts.

Hopefully, you can see how prompts get you started but don't do all the work for you. You will need to use your knowledge, experience and perhaps a bit of imagination to complete your piece.

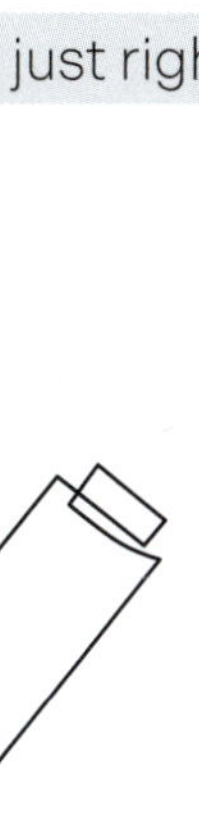

ISBN: 9780170499286

Have a go ...

Now it's time for you to practise putting a plan together using prompts. Read the question below and complete the following tasks.

QUESTION: Formal letter

Your school's Canteen Manager has asked for student suggestions for changes to the canteen's menu.

Write a formal letter to your school's Canteen Manager to explain what suggestions you have to make sure that all students can buy food to suit their needs.

Write between 150 and 250 words.

You should:

- introduce yourself.

You might mention:

- more options
- cultural food differences
- personal likes/dislikes.
- healthy foods
- cost for families

Remember, you will be marked on: length, ideas, structure, language, audience, purpose, accuracy. See page 70 for more detail.

School's dramatic canteen revamp

Business is booming at a Dunedin school's canteen since its menu was given a healthy overhaul.

Pies, chips, lollies and fizzy drinks have been kicked for touch at Bayfield High School. These days, you'll find students tucking into freshly-made sandwiches, salads and wraps.

Not only are students eating better food but the Dunedin school's canteen is now making more money in a day than it previously did in a week!

But revamping the canteen has been no walk in the park; it's demanded a year-long team effort involving students, staff and the Heart Foundation.

It all started when students and staff decided early last year that their school food was unappealing and unhealthy. It was time for change.

A student health team got busy surveying students to gauge their thoughts on the matter and ask for healthy food suggestions.

The team then presented their ideas at the local Health Promoting Schools network meeting, winning the competition for best ideas and presentation on the day.

PLANNING STEP 1

Annotate the question in the same way as you learnt to do on page 71.

PLANNING STEP 2

Let's use the prompts to help come up with some ideas. We have given a few. Now you add more.

Prompt	Ideas
Introduce myself	
More options	*wraps ...*
Healthy foods	*vegetarian, low sugar ...*
Cost for families	*price under $10 ...*
Cultural food differences	*halal, rice ...*
Personal likes and dislikes	*chips ...*

Which three do you think you can explain the best? Remember, each idea should have its own paragraph. Which paragraph/idea should go first, second and then third?

 ISBN: 9780170499286

Time to write

SEND ▷

TO: jfrancis@watersidehigh.school.nz

SUBJECT: Feedback on canteen menu.

Introduction

Dear Mrs Francis

Thank you for asking for student feedback about the canteen's menu. My name is ________ ________ and I am a Year 11 student here at Waterside High School. I would like to make some suggestions for changes that I believe will be good for students.

Paragraph 1
More choice

Firstly,

Paragraph 2
Healthy and less expensive

Secondly,

Paragraph 3
Different cultural needs

Thirdly,

Conclusion

Thank you for the opportunity to make these suggestions for changes to the canteen menu. I would be happy to discuss them further with you.

Kind regards,

....

Let's now look at ways to help you meet the word count ...

ISBN: 9780170499286

Write to the word count

Planning what ideas, examples and details you will use in your writing will help you reach the minimum word count without repeating your ideas.

How might this part of an assessment go wrong?

- *Student does not meet minimum word count.*
- *Student meets word count but repeats same idea without expanding or building on it.*

Here are a few simple ways to ensure that you write enough.

1 Use the question and the prompts

There will be several ideas for you to build on.

2 Add examples

For example, if you write ***food should be tasty***, add information about which foods you like the taste of.

Compare the length of these sentences:

a *Food should taste good. I particularly enjoy spicy food such as Thai green curry, samosas and sushi with wasabi paste.* (20 words)

b *Food should taste good. I particularly enjoy spicy food.* (9 words)

Example **a** not only gives the reader a clearer idea of what the writer means by spicy, but it is also more than twice as long as example **b**. Providing examples works!

3 Use what you know

You might be surprised by what you already know about the topic. Think about:

- personal experience
- information from a school subject like Science, Economics or Health/PE
- something that has happened in your family or group of friends
- a place, event or activity in your community
- something you know about from the wider world
- information you have read online or in a book.

4 Make up believable details

You will not be able to look up quotes or statistics. It's acceptable to invent some just for these tasks.

Trying to prove a point?

Make up a **believable** statistic. Like this: *In a recent Waterside High School survey, 17% of respondents said the canteen doesn't sell food they will eat.*

Need an expert quote? Make it up!

Taylor Martin, researcher at the University of Rockville, found that students feel more connected to a place if they can purchase food they like at the school canteen.

ISBN: 9780170499286

Let's take a closer look at how to write more …

Look at this brainstorm to see how a student thought about a topic before beginning to write.

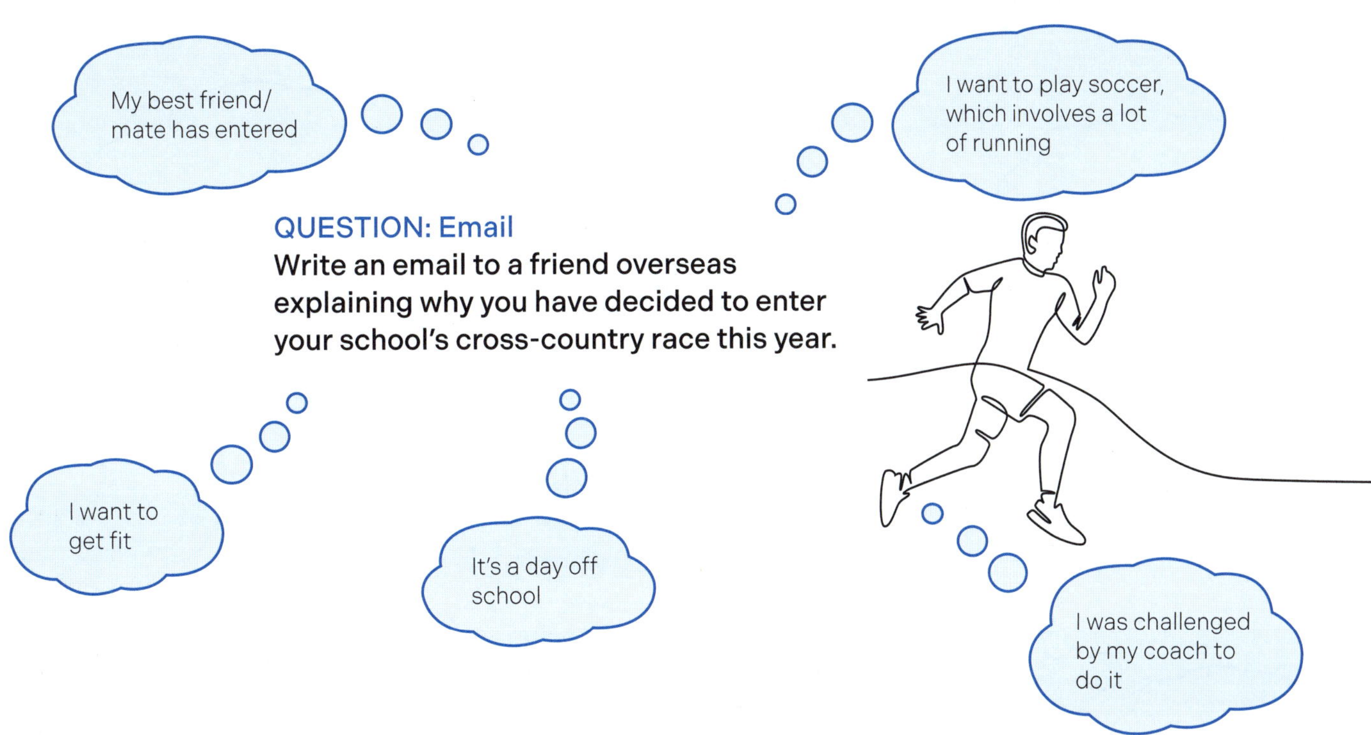

The student then added extra details from their studies and personal experience.
Remember, you can invent believable and relevant ideas.
This does not have to be about you personally!

My best friend/ mate has entered

I feel nervous that I might have to walk a lot of it

I want to play soccer, which involves a lot of running

Read a blog by an NZ cross-country runner who travels the world now

Best mate is very persuasive

QUESTION: Email

Write an email to a friend overseas explaining why you have decided to enter your school's cross-country race this year.

I want to get fit

It's a day off school

I was challenged by my coach to do it

Getting fit enough to run is good for my body and mind (Health/PE)

I ran a Round the Bays run last year (personal experience)

We'll circle back to this question later.

Have a go ...

Take a look at the question below and have a go at brainstorming your own ideas based on the prompts provided and what you already know.

QUESTION: Article

Everyone in your class has been asked to write an article for the school newspaper.

Your topic is: **Learning to cook is a good idea**

Write between 250 and 350 words.

In your answer, possible ideas include:

- understanding how meals are created
- helping at home
- following recipes and managing quantities
- being self-sufficient
- eating what you enjoy.

We'll circle back to this question later.

Have another go ...

Here is an example of a student piece of writing that does not meet the minimum count. They were supposed to write at least 150 words.

The question was:

QUESTION: Email

Write an email to an exchange student who is moving to the place where you live. Tell them what there is for teenagers to enjoy.

Write between 150 and 250 words.

In your answer, you could mention:

- popular places for teenagers
- activities or events they might enjoy
- tips for helping them get around.

 ISBN: 9780170499286

Hi Hiroto	
You will be moving here soon so I thought I'd tell you a bit about this place.	INTRODUCTION
There is a town centre with a few shops and a community centre for meetings and events.	PARAGRAPH 1
We've got a skatepark and a swimming pool. Other games are played on the local park grounds. You will be able to keep playing rugby.	PARAGRAPH 2
We have a library where there are plenty of computers. I go there quite often as I can work there.	PARAGRAPH 3
There is also a bit of forest close to town and it's got mountain bike tracks.	PARAGRAPH 4
You'll like it here. I do.	CONCLUSION
From Peta	

This is 105 words. It needs an additional 50 at least. Look back at the list on page 84 under 'Use what you know' to get ideas for how this can be expanded.

Write four sentences of examples to add to paragraphs 1, 2, 3 and 4 to bring this writing up to the minimum word count.

PARAGRAPH 1	
PARAGRAPH 2	
PARAGRAPH 3	
PARAGRAPH 4	

How many words have you added to the email? ☐ + 105 = ☐

Now you've learnt to create ideas, let's look at putting them into paragraphs ...

Use paragraphs

Why do paragraphs matter?

- Paragraphs help the reader follow your ideas by showing when you're moving from one idea to the next.
- Paragraphs keep your writing focused, as each paragraph has **one** main idea.
- Paragraphs help you plan and organise your writing, so you don't forget anything important.

> **How might this part of an assessment go wrong?**
> - *Student forgets to use paragraphs.*
> - *Writing is a jumble of ideas and therefore difficult to read.*

You have been writing in paragraphs for years. You may have learned this acronym or one similar:

TEEC

• **T**opic sentence	Start with a clear sentence that tells the reader what your paragraph is about (topic).
• **E**xample	Give a real, or realistic, example to support your topic.
• **E**xplanation	Explain how your example supports your topic and why it matters (aim for two sentences).
• **C**onclusion	End with a sentence that sums up your main point or shows why it is important.

Let's take a closer look at paragraphing

Highlight/annotate each of these four parts (TEEC) in each of the paragraphs below.

Paragraph A

Wearing a school uniform helps students feel like they belong. For example, when everyone wears the same clothes, there's less pressure to dress a certain way or wear expensive brands. This creates a more relaxed environment because students don't have to worry about being judged for what they wear. They can concentrate on learning and friendships instead of fitting in. Overall, uniforms can make school an easier place to be.

ISBN: 9780170499286

Paragraph B

One way our school could help reduce plastic is by encouraging students to use reusable water bottles. For example, we could install more water fountains or refill stations around the school to make it easier for students to top up their bottles. This would help reduce the number of single-use plastic bottles being brought to school and thrown away. Over time, it would also help students build better habits around reusing and recycling. Making this small change could have a big impact on the amount of plastic our school uses.

Have a go …

Using the information below, create your own TEEC paragraph.

1 a Choose one of the following paragraph starters:

- One way our school could be more environmentally friendly is …
- A school rule I would change is …
- School camps are valuable because …

b Use the space below to brainstorm an idea you could write about. Remember, you'll be using only one idea to write one paragraph, so choose something you feel confident explaining in detail.

BRAINSTORM

THINK: What do I know about this topic?

Starter: ______________________________

c Now, use your brainstorm to create your own Topic, Example, Explanation, Conclusion (TEEC) paragraph in the template provided.

Use the sentence starters below to help if you get stuck.

Topic One way we could ... Something that would help is ...	
Example For example, ... One way this could work is ...	
Explanation This would help because ... This means that ...	
Conclusion Overall, this would ... This change would make a big difference because ...	

d Reread your paragraph and check:

Did I stay focused on one main idea? Yes / No

Did I give an example? Yes / No

Did I explain it clearly? Yes / No

Did I finish with a conclusion? Yes / No

Linking paragraphs together ...
Following an acronym like TEEC makes sure every paragraph is made of sentences that link together.

Then all you have to do is make sure that the paragraphs are in a sequence that develops your thoughts from the opening statement to the concluding words of your piece of writing.

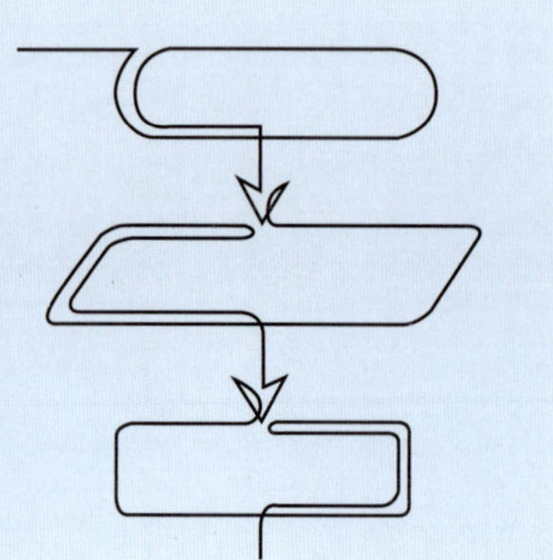

Let's look at how to organise your paragraphs ...

 ISBN: 9780170499286

WRITING FOCUS 6

Organise your writing

Every good piece of writing needs a beginning, a middle and an end.

How might this part of an assessment go wrong?
- *Student's ideas are not in a logical sequence.*
- *Student does not use paragraphing.*

BEGINNING

The **introduction** sets up your topic, shows your opinion about the topic and may state your main idea. Opening words could be:

- Everyone knows that ...
- I believe that ...
- Would you believe that ...
- It is true that ...

In the introduction, you should use words taken directly from the question to keep your writing on track.

MIDDLE

The **body paragraphs** are where you explain your points in detail, using examples or evidence in the TEEC structure.

The easiest way to introduce each paragraph is to use the words 'Firstly', 'Secondly' and 'Thirdly' (and 'Fourthly') to start each paragraph.

END

The **conclusion** ties it all together and reminds the reader what your main point was.

The easiest way to start a conclusion is: 'Finally, ...'

Why does structure matter?

- It stops you from jumping around between ideas.
- It ensures you stick to your plan, so you don't get lost halfway through.
- It makes sure you actually answer the question fully, and that your ideas make sense to the person reading your writing.

Let's take a closer look at how a student's writing was improved by using better structure

The student was answering the following question as a practice for their Literacy Writing assessment.

QUESTION: Article

Your school or community group is putting together a resource for people who are new to the area.

Write an article describing ONE place or experience you think new community members would enjoy.

Write between 150 and 250 words.

In your answer, you must:
- write about just one place or experience.

In your answer, possible ideas include:
- think about what makes it enjoyable
- what you need to bring
- what it costs.

STUDENT'S FIRST ATTEMPT

The Treetop Bridge at Kauri Glen Reserve is cool and people should go there because it's high up and you can see heaps of trees and birds and there's a boardwalk too that goes through the bush. I went there with my cousin and we liked how it felt like walking in the air. It's good for new people because it's not far away and it's free and you don't need to be super fit to walk it. There are signs and stuff about the bush and trees which is good if you like nature. It might be a bit scary if you're afraid of heights but it's not that bad. I think new people in Birkenhead should go check it out.

Did this student do any thinking and planning or did they just write down anything and everything that came to mind?

Notice that:
- the whole text is just one paragraph
- there are ideas but they are all jumbled with no detail provided
- there's no introduction or conclusion
- there are informal words like 'heaps', 'stuff', 'go check it out'
- it reads like the student is just putting down their disorganised thoughts.

ISBN: 9780170499286

STUDENT'S SECOND ATTEMPT

The same student tried again.

This time they:

- looked at the prompts again
- thought about the three main ideas they wanted to communicate
- decided what they could write in most detail about
- spent some time planning the structure of their text: firstly, secondly, finally
- chose more formal words.

Here is the result of this process.

> *One place I think new people in Birkenhead should visit is the new Treetop Bridge and boardwalk at Kauri Glen Reserve. It's a great way to experience the local bush and learn more about the area. It is also free and easy for all ages.*
>
> *Firstly, I think Kauri Glen Reserve is a good place to visit because it is surrounded by nature. It gives people the chance to enjoy the outdoors in a calm and peaceful setting. For example, you can walk above the trees on the bridge, and it feels like you're right up in the forest canopy. You can see birds, hear the sounds of the bush, and there are signs that tell you about the trees and plants. It's a peaceful spot that helps people feel connected to the natural environment.*
>
> *Secondly, it's an easy and free activity for all ages. You don't have to be super fit to do the walk, and it's close to town. It's easy because the paths and boardwalk are well made, so they're easy to walk on, and it's a safe place to explore. It's also a nice spot for families or people new to the area who want to get outside without going too far.*
>
> *Finally, I think the Treetop Bridge and boardwalk at Kauri Glen Reserve is a special place that new community members would enjoy. It's relaxing, interesting, and shows off the beauty of Birkenhead.*

Hopefully, you can see very clearly that the second attempt is far superior to the first!

YOU DO:

Use four different-coloured pens and identify:

- the **beginning** (what is the topic?)
- the **middle** (all the ideas or details)
- the **end** (does it have a wrap-up or conclusion?)
- **sequencing** words ('Firstly', 'Secondly', ...).

Have a go ...

We've looked at how to organise a piece of writing – now it's time for you to practise creating your own structured plan. A strong structured plan helps make sure your ideas are organised in a clear and logical way, which makes your writing easier for the reader to follow.

Read the question on the following page, then use the prompts and your own experiences to complete the planning template.

QUESTION: Email

Your local cycle path has not been repaired for two years.

Write an email to your local Council Environmental Officer, Alan Mauga, explaining **what** is wrong and **why** you think it should be looked after more regularly.

Give your email the subject line: Waterview Cycle Path Needs Help

Write between 150 and 250 words.

You might include:

- current problems for cyclists
- how the path used to be
- what you think should be done
- what benefits there would be to repairing the path.

Remember, you did some thinking on this question on page 75.

STRUCTURED PLAN	
Introduction	
Body paragraph 1	
Body paragraph 2	
Body paragraph 3	
Conclusion	

YOU DO:

- Evaluate your **plan**.
- Check it is addressed to the correct person.
- Have you got three **different but linked** ideas? Maybe past, present, future.
- Have you got a specific example to back up each idea?
- Have you covered all or most of the suggested prompts?

Now let's look at some common writing challenges.

ISBN: 9780170499286

WRITING FOCUS 7

Know when to stop ...

One problem that many students have with their writing is the **run-on sentence** – essentially, they don't know when to stop.

How might this part of an assessment go wrong?

- *Student confuses the reader with long, jumbled sentences.*
- *Student doesn't identify where one idea ends and another begins.*
- *Student doesn't use full stops to create more natural, readable writing.*

Let's take a closer look at run-on sentences

A run-on sentence is a sentence that contains more than one idea without proper punctuation.

Most teenagers hate getting up in the morning in winter it's dark and cold and they like keeping warm in bed and sleeping in.

Ask yourself: Do these teenagers hate getting up every morning or just in winter? Better punctuation – just one full stop and a capital letter – would make this clear.

Most teenagers hate getting up in the ***morning. In*** *winter it's dark and cold and they like keeping warm in bed and sleeping in.*

Answer: Yes, they hate getting up every morning.

Where else could the full stop go in this sentence?

Have a go ...

1 Using a red pen, add full stops and capital letters to turn these single-sentence paragraphs into **several shorter sentences**. You will need to remove the word 'and' in some places – just break the paragraphs into clear, simple sentences that make sense.

a *Yesterday we had netball trials at school and it was really hot outside so everyone got tired really fast and some people forgot to bring water so they felt sick we had to stop early but I still think I did pretty well and I hope I get into the team.*

b *I think the school should create a new leadership role where students who are good with technology can help others because some students struggle with things like logging in or using Google Docs they miss out on learning time while waiting for help from the teacher and if we had trained tech leaders they could help straight away it would make everything run more smoothly plus it gives the tech students a chance to show leadership and build their confidence*

ISBN: 9780170499286

2 Here are TWO paragraphs, each of which has a run-on sentence. They have been highlighted for you. Rewrite each run-on sentence in the space provided. Try to make the ideas easier to understand. You may change the punctuation and move, remove or add words as you please.

A *I think school uniforms are a good idea because everyone looks the same and there's less pressure to wear expensive clothes.* ***Some students don't like them, they say they hate the colours and they hate the skirts and the shoes are uncomfortable and they should be free to choose their own clothes and school uniform is boring.*** *In my opinion uniforms are a good thing because I don't have to think about what to wear every day.*

B *I think having a pet would be really fun.* ***It teaches you to be responsible and pets like dogs and cats need food and walks and attention and if you forget and don't look after them right they can get sad or sick and they are messy but make good friends****. I want a dog but my mother says we don't have enough space and it would be too much work for her.*

Now you can recognise run-on sentences, take care with your own work to make sure they don't appear. Read your work, aloud if possible, to help you spot where some might be hiding.

Now let's look at using the right words at the right times ...

 ISBN: 9780170499286

Use appropriate language

In the Literacy Writing assessment you must use formal polite language if you wish to pass the assessment. Think of the language you use when talking or writing to a respected adult (your principal, your teacher, your koru, your aunt, your coach) compared with talking or writing to a friend.

This means:

- no slang
- no short phrases
- no colloquial words
- no swearing
- avoiding most contractions.

How might this part of an assessment go wrong?

- *Student writes in language that is too casual.*
- *Student does not use formal English.*

The following words are some that you should avoid in your writing:

wanna (want to)
gonna (going to)
gimme (give me)
dunno (don't know)
reckon (think)
cos/cus/cause (because)
kinda (kind of)
sorta (sort of)

stuff (things/items)
like (such as)
yous (you, you all)
heaps (a lot)
cool (great)
real good (really good)
sweet (good)
nah (no)

bro (mate/friend)
gutted (disappointed)
chur (thanks)
legit (legitimate/genuine/seriously)
flash (fancy/stylish)

All you have to do is NOT write in the casual language you might use speaking to a friend who is the same age as you.

Let's take a look at two examples ...

Example 1

Read this sentence aloud. It might sound fine if you were chatting to a friend.

I'm gonna tell youse 'bout my experience of epic fishing.

For a piece of formal writing, it has slang ('epic'), contractions ('I'm', 'gonna', ''bout') and a dialect/colloquial pronoun ('youse').

If the student changes these words to more formal words, they would be fine.

***I am going to** tell **you about** my experience of **successful** fishing.*

Example 2

Read this sentence aloud. It might sound fine if you were chatting to a friend.

> *Josh and me went to the beach yesterday and it was wicked but an old guy threw a wobbly cos we dropped some bombs off the wharf.*

For a piece of formal writing, it has slang ('wicked', 'threw a wobbly', 'old guy', 'dropped some bombs'), a contraction ('cos') and wrong pronoun ('me').

If the student changes these words to more formal words, they would be fine.

> *Josh and **I** went to the beach yesterday and it was **excellent** but an old **man got angry with us because** we **jumped off** the wharf **several times.***

Have a go ...

Correct the following sentences. Highlight the casual language and then rewrite the sentence more formally.

1 *I just wanna say thanks for the new hoops — they're way better now, reckon the whole neighbourhood loves them.*

____

____

____

2 *Reckon we're gonna hit the beach this arvo, but I'm kinda worried it might rain.*

____

____

____

3 *That concert was real good, the band was sweet, and the crowd was heaps loud.*

____

____

____

YOU DO:

In the box write any colloquial and slang words that you use. Ask your teacher and/or caregiver and/or friend if they agree with you. Would they add any?

These are the words YOU must avoid in the Writing assessment! You might add to this list as you (or your teachers) notice other colloquial words in your writing.

Let's look at the final step — proofreading and checking for clarity.

 ISBN: 9780170499286

Proofreading – your final step

The Writing assessment is asking you to write formally, with care and accuracy. Taking a little time to read through and check your completed work is great advice. You may be surprised at the corrections you are able to make for yourself.

How might this part of an assessment go wrong?
• *Student does not check their work for any errors in spelling, punctuation, sentences, grammar or paragraphing.*

Checking our own writing is not so easy because we tend to read what we *think* we wrote. However, you can help yourself by reading your words 'aloud in your head'.

Content checklist:

- Does my writing make sense?
- Is it organised into paragraphs?
- Does it use sequencing words to link paragraphs?
- Does it say all I want to say on the topic?
- Does it use samples to support my ideas?
- Is it long enough?

Proofreading checklist:

- Is there a capital letter at the start of every sentence?
- Have I used capital letters for names of people, places and businesses?
- Is there a full stop at the end of every sentence?
- Have I written any run-on sentences?
- Is my spelling okay? Have I used any available spell check?
- Can I change words I'm not sure how to spell to a simpler word?
- Have I used formal language?
- Have I used any slang or too casual words?
- Have I written in a polite way?

Let's take a closer look at proofreading

Admittedly, these days AI is doing our proofreading for us. However, this Literacy Writing assessment is asking you to prove that you can be your own proofreader and make your words as polished and perfect as possible, all by yourself!

Let's look at a piece of writing that shows the many mistakes a student can make. We've exaggerated the mistakes – we're sure you'll see that the writing can be improved very easily.

Below is a text that a student wrote for their assessment answering this question.

QUESTION: Email

Write an email to your principal **explaining an idea you have for a fundraiser for Gumboot Friday**, an organisation that supports free counselling of young people in New Zealand.

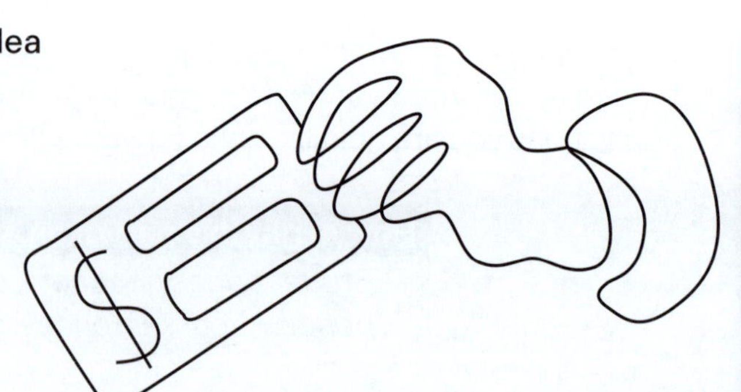

Aim to write between 150 and 250 words.

You might include:

- reasons for fundraising
- why students would enjoy the activity
- how it fits in with school time
- why you are making this particular suggestion.

STUDENT ANSWER

I rekon we should do some kinda fundrayser for Gumboot friday cos it's a good cause and people are like struggling with mental health. Everybody knows some one who needs help and this shows we care about other people.

We could maybe do a bake sail or wear gumboots to school or somethink like that. Theres heaps of people who wanna help but dont know how eh.

i rekon loads of students woold join in to make this a grate event. My class would get involved and dress up and bring food and have a good time it could happen over lunchtime or in the afternoon

Also its fun and makes winter a bit more cheerful and it shows we care and its a good idea for the school to do.

Clearly, this piece of writing would not pass. Can you work out why?

Use different-coloured pens/highlighters to identify:

- casual language or slang
- missing full stops
- run-on sentence
- length
- introduction?
- missing capital letters
- missing apostrophes
- spelling errors
- heading?
- conclusion?

If you need to be reminded about some of these things, check pages 47–54.

Have a go ...

You can do a lot better than this. On the next page, rewrite the student's email. Make it more formal. Make it more accurate. Give it a clear introduction, three body paragraphs and a conclusion.

Then, check your work! Use the checklist again to make sure you have not made any of the same mistakes.

ISBN: 9780170499286

SEND

TO

SUBJECT

Footnote:

If you are writing by hand, you may have to add extra refill pages. If you are typing your writing on a computer rather than in this book, then printing the page is a good idea.

CHECK YOUR WORK

- Does my text make sense?
- Does it say all I want to say on the topic?
- Is it long enough?
- Is it organised into paragraphs?
- Is there a capital letter and full stop for every sentence?
- Have I fixed any run-on sentences?
- Have I checked my spelling?
- Have I used formal language?

For more reminders, see page 99.

Let's write together

For each of the following three questions, we have provided help to get you started. We know that beginning a piece of writing can be the hard part, but it's best to take time to think and plan before you put pen to paper. This means you will write more easily, you should meet the required length with ease, and you will have time to check the accuracy of your writing when you have finished.

QUESTION: Blog

Write a blog post for your school's intranet in its section called *Making the Most of School*. You have been asked to **encourage students to eat breakfast at home regularly**.

Write between 150 and 250 words.

You might mention:

- energy and concentration benefits
- good food = better health = better attendance
- less costly than shop-bought food
- easy choices save time
- family time is healthy, too.

Remember, you will be marked on: length, ideas, structure, language, audience, purpose, accuracy. See page 70 for more detail.

PLANNING STEP 1

Annotate the question in the same way as you learnt to do on page 71.

PLANNING STEP 2

We've provided a possible structure for your three body paragraphs using the TEEC format (see page 88). However, feel free to include your own ideas or points, as this will help make your writing more personal.

Paragraph 1: Energy and focus	*Paragraph 2: Health and nutrition*	*Paragraph 3: It's easy to fit in*
T: *Breakfast gives you energy and focus*	T: *Eat and stay healthy*	T: *A little is better than nothing*
E: *Can concentrate better*	E: *Fruit, cereal or toast for fibre*	E: *Banana, cereal or toast is quick and easy*
E: *No food makes us tired quickly*	E: *Skipping breakfast, eat poorly later*	E: *Breakfast can be fast or eaten on the go*
C: *Any morning food good*	C: *Healthy food first means better health and more time at school to learn*	C: *Everyone can find time to fit it in*

 ISBN: 9780170499286

TIME TO WRITE

The introductory paragraph and the conclusion have been written for you. All you have to do is follow the plan and finish the writing.

EAT BREAKFAST EVERY DAY

Intro

We have all come to school without breakfast at one time or another. This is not a good idea. Breakfast is a very important meal and every student at Oceanview High School should eat something before they begin their school day. By doing this, they will make the most of school.

food = energy = concentration

In the first place, everyone understands that ...

Secondly,

Thirdly,

Conclusion

Finally, it is clear that students who eat breakfast of some sort every day function better at school. Look around you. Who do you think had breakfast this morning? They are the ones who have more energy, can concentrate and are in better health than the others. Eat breakfast, stay healthy and make the most of school.

CHECK YOUR WORK

- Does my text make sense?
- Does it say all I want to say on the topic?
- Is it long enough?
- Is it organised into paragraphs?
- Is there a capital letter and full stop for every sentence?
- Have I fixed any run-on sentences?
- Have I checked my spelling?
- Have I used formal language?

For more reminders, see page 99.

QUESTION: Formal letter

You have been involved in a project at school to encourage reducing waste.

Write a letter to your local mayor explaining what your school has done and why it is important for your local community to do the same.

Write between 150 and 250 words.

Some possible ideas you could include are:

- reduce: buy less
- reuse and repair: shop for second-hand clothes and other pre-owned items
- recycle all electronic and plastic waste.

In your answer, you could:

- give examples of your school's actions that reduce waste
- describe how these actions make/made a difference
- explain why not just young people should get involved.

Remember, you will be marked on: length, ideas, structure, language, audience, purpose, accuracy. See page 70 for more detail.

PLANNING STEP 1

Annotate the question in the same way as you learnt to do on page 71.

PLANNING STEP 2

To the right is a student's brainstorm. Add any of your own ideas and then look at how you can group the ideas together to make different paragraphs. Which points could be for the introduction, three body paragraphs and conclusion?

- *Local tip full of waste, glass, paper, electrical — better if recycled*
- *Reuse: started a uniform exchange, hold a swap shop once a term*
- *Mend: I look after my bike in workshop to keep it going*
- *Recycle: paper, plastic containers*
- *School had lots of waste like canteen and tech and paper waste — decided on a plan to reduce*
- *Compost and paper recycling — much less rubbish around, feels good, pride*
- *Better for school, so better for community — everyone needs to reduce, reuse, recycle*

THINK: What do I know about this topic?

Add your own ideas here:

Introduction:

Body paragraph 1:

Body paragraph 2:

Body paragraph 3:

Conclusion:

 ISBN: 9780170499286

TIME TO WRITE

For this writing, we have provided a starter phrase for each paragraph.

Dear ______________________

I want to share with you my school's efforts ______________________

____

____

Our biggest problem was ______________________

____

____

____

____

____

____

Another thing that we tackled was ______________________

____

____

____

____

____

____

Overall, I think we achieved a ______________________

____

____

____

____

____

____

____

In conclusion, ______________________

____

Yours sincerely, ______________________

CHECK YOUR WORK

- Does my text make sense?
- Does it say all I want to say on the topic?
- Is it long enough?
- Is it organised into paragraphs?
- Is there a capital letter and full stop for every sentence?
- Have I fixed any run-on sentences?
- Have I checked my spelling?
- Have I used formal language?

For more reminders, see page 99.

QUESTION: Article

Write an article for your community newspaper. You have been asked to explain to your community **why gaming can be a positive part of teenage life**.

You **should** explain:

- what gaming is
- why adults worry about the time spent on it by teenagers.

You **might** mention:

- skills
- friendship and teamwork
- confidence
- learning.

Write between 250 and 350 words.

Remember, you will be marked on: length, ideas, structure, language, audience, purpose, accuracy. See page 70 for more detail.

PLANNING STEP 1

Annotate the question in the same way as you learnt to do on page 71. Note the longer word count.

PLANNING STEP 2

Read through the ideas carefully. There is enough material here to give you three ideas for the three body paragraphs you will write. However, add you own ideas if you have any.

Gaming helps develop important skills

- Problem-solving, thinking quickly, decision-making.
- Involves strategy, logic, fast reactions.
- Minecraft = creativity and planning, while action games require quick thinking.

Gaming builds friendships and teamwork

- Multiplayer games = communication and teamwork to succeed.
- Examples? Fortnite or Roblox?
- Help even outside of gaming.

Gaming builds confidence and helps with learning

- Complete levels or improve in a game = sense of achievement.
- Teens feel proud of themselves.
- More motivated to try new things.

ISBN: 9780170499286

TIME TO WRITE

More lines over the page ...

CHECK YOUR WORK

- Does my text make sense?
- Does it say all I want to say on the topic?
- Is it long enough?
- Is it organised into paragraphs?
- Is there a capital letter and full stop for every sentence?
- Have I fixed any run-on sentences?
- Have I checked my spelling?
- Have I used formal language?

For more reminders, see page 99.

Footnote:
If you are writing by hand, you may have to add extra refill pages. If you are typing your writing on a computer rather than in this book, then printing the page is a good idea.

ISBN: 9780170499286

Your turn

You are now ready to answer a Literacy Writing question by yourself. Just remember the essentials:

- Read the question and the instructions carefully.
- Use the prompts.
- Write to the word count.
- Use examples and explanations.
- Use formal English.
- Proofread your work.

QUESTION: Email

Write an email to your school's principal about why students should, or should not, be allowed to listen to music in class while working on a device.

Write between 150 and 250 words.

Remember, you will be marked on: length, ideas, structure, language, audience, purpose, accuracy. See page 70 for more detail.

Possible ideas include:

+		−	
 	• Find it relaxing • Stops other distractions • Learning to focus • Enjoyable • Good practice for other places that have background music	− −	• Distracting • Can miss instructions/explanations • Inappropriate lyrics if choosing own • Not everyone has headphones • Teacher doesn't know what you are listening to • Can't hear teacher, or fire alarm

PLANNING STEP 1

Annotate the question in the same way as you learnt to do on page 71.

PLANNING STEP 2

ISBN: 9780170499286

TIME TO WRITE

CHECK YOUR WORK

- Does my text make sense?
- Does it say all I want to say on the topic?
- Is it long enough?
- Is it organised into paragraphs?
- Is there a capital letter and full stop for every sentence?
- Have I fixed any run-on sentences?
- Have I checked my spelling?
- Have I used formal language?

For more reminders, see page 99.

Footnote:
If you are writing by hand, you may have to add extra refill pages. If you are typing your writing on a computer rather than in this book, then printing the page is a good idea.

ISBN: 9780170499286

5

QUESTION: Article

Your school has banned mobile phone use during school hours, including break times.

Write an article for your school newsletter **explaining the benefits of this new rule and how it's helping students**.

Write between 250 and 350 words.

You might like to write about:

- What changed when phones were banned?
- How has it helped students focus in class?
- Has it improved social interaction or break-time behaviour?
- What are teachers noticing since the ban?
- Why is this rule good for learning and wellbeing?

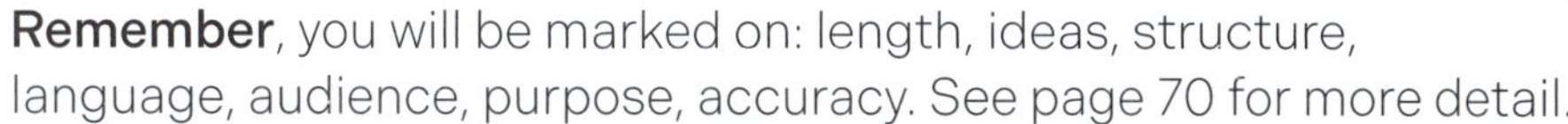

Remember, you will be marked on: length, ideas, structure, language, audience, purpose, accuracy. See page 70 for more detail.

PLANNING STEP 1

Annotate the question in the same way as you learnt to do on page 71.

PLANNING STEP 2

TIME TO WRITE

ISBN: 9780170499286

Footnote:
If you are writing by hand, you may have to add extra refill pages. If you are typing your writing on a computer rather than in this book, then printing the page is a good idea.

CHECK YOUR WORK

- Does my text make sense?
- Does it say all I want to say on the topic?
- Is it long enough?
- Is it organised into paragraphs?
- Is there a capital letter and full stop for every sentence?
- Have I fixed any run-on sentences?
- Have I checked my spelling?
- Have I used formal language?

For more reminders, see page 99.

QUESTION: Advice column

You have been asked to write a response to the email written by local teenager Kerry asking for advice:

> *I am 15 years old. I live with my mum and my little brother in an apartment. Is it a good idea for me to get a pet?*

Decide whether you will answer **yes** or **no** and write your response accordingly.

Your response will be published in your local newspaper's online *Ask Auntie* column.

Write between 150 and 250 words.

Possible ideas include:

+		−	
+	• responsibility • companionship • compassion • activity • personal experience	−	• time commitment • moving away from home • cost • not ready for responsibility • personal experience

Remember, you will be marked on: length, ideas, structure, language, audience, purpose, accuracy. See page 70 for more detail.

PLANNING STEP 1

Annotate the question in the same way as you learnt to do on page 71.

PLANNING STEP 2

 ISBN: 9780170499286

TIME TO WRITE

CHECK YOUR WORK

- Does my text make sense?
- Does it say all I want to say on the topic?
- Is it long enough?
- Is it organised into paragraphs?
- Is there a capital letter and full stop for every sentence?
- Have I fixed any run-on sentences?
- Have I checked my spelling?
- Have I used formal language?

For more reminders, see page 99.

Footnote:

If you are writing by hand, you may have to add extra refill pages. If you are typing your writing on a computer rather than in this book, then printing the page is a good idea.

The more you practise, the easier it gets

Throughout this workbook, you have worked with many Literacy Writing assessment-style questions. Sometimes you have brainstormed ideas, sometimes you have written only a plan or a single paragraph, and other times you have practised skills such as annotating and proofreading.

In the table on the following page, there is a list of all the topics in the Writing section you have not yet written a full answer for. You will see this icon identifying these topics.
It is a very good idea to use these topics for extra writing practice.

Go back to each of the questions
Review the notes, plans and activities you completed earlier for that question.
Use the work you have already done to help you write a complete response for each question.

Write each answer as though you are sitting the real assessment:

- Follow the question's instructions carefully.
- Use the skills you have practised throughout this section.
- Write as careful and detailed a response as possible.
- Check your work as if you are handing it in for marking.

When you have finished, read your work aloud. You cannot do this in a formal assessment, but you can when you are practising. This is the best way to check for yourself that your writing keeps to the topic, is sensible and flows well.

  ISBN: 9780170499286

	Question	Work completed	Tick when complete
Page 72	Your school is starting a work experience programme for senior students. Write a letter to a local business (real or imagined) in your area (e.g. a café, mechanic, hair salon, vet, office) asking if they would be interested in hosting a student for a short work placement.	Question annotated.	
Page 75 and 94	Your local cycle path has not been repaired for two years. Write an email to your local Council Environmental Officer, Alan Mauga, explaining what is wrong and why you think it should be looked after more regularly. Give your email the subject line: Waterview Cycle Path Needs Help	Question annotated, planning done.	
Page 85	Write an email to a friend overseas explaining why you have decided to enter your school's cross-country race this year.	Prompts provided.	
Page 86	Everyone in your class has been asked to write an article for the school newspaper. Your topic is: Learning to cook is a good idea	Ideas created by you.	
Page 86	Write an email to an exchange student who is moving to the place where you live. Tell them what there is for teenagers to enjoy.	You added to another person's example. Now write an answer based on your own community.	
Page 92	Your school or community group is putting together a resource for people who are new to the area. Write an article describing ONE place or experience you think new community members would enjoy.	Review the samples. Then base your answer on your own community.	

Congratulations, you've completed this workbook and you're well on your way to passing the Literacy Reading and Writing assessments ...

ISBN: 9780170499286

Practice set 8 (page 62)

1 C
2 D
3 C
4 A
5 B
6 A
7 C
8 Two, to

Practice set 9 (page 63)

1 C
2 D
3 C
4 A
5 taller, better
6 A
7 sea, Its
8 D

Practice set 10 (page 64)

1 D
2 C
3 C
4 B
5 C
6 We're, where
7 D
8 C

Practice set 11 (page 65)

1 C
2 C
3 D
4 because
5 B
6 C
7 C
8 B

Practice set 12 (page 66)

1 C
2 B
3 B
4 A
5 B
6 D
7 B
8 quiet, beautifully

Practice set 13 (page 67)

1 C
2 D
3 so
4 A
5 A
6 C
7 C
8 C

Practice set 14 (page 68)

1 D
2 unless
3 D
4 C
5 B
6 C
7 D
8 B

Practice set 15 (page 69)

1 D
2 A
3 A
4 B
5 B
6 C
7 dessert
8 A

Let's get writing

It's difficult to assess your own writing. If these writing tasks are being done through school, a teacher will check your writing for you as part of your preparation for the Literacy Writing assessment.

If you are doing the writing tasks independently, politely ask a teacher or someone else you know is good with words to read what you have written and give you feedback on how well you have communicated your ideas.

Always complete your own check first by reading the finished piece through with critical eyes.

Writing focus 7: Know when to stop ... (pages 95–96)

Possible answers:

A Some students don't like school uniforms because they say they are boring. They say they hate the colour and the skirts. They say the shoes are uncomfortable, too. They want to be free to choose their own clothes every day.

B Having a pet teaches you to be responsible because any pet needs to be given food, exercise and attention. Pets like dogs and cats can get sad or sick if their owners don't look after them properly. It's true that pets can be messy but they are also good friends to any family.

Writing focus 8: Use appropriate language (pages 97–98)

Possible answers:

1 I just **want to** say **thank you** for the new hoops. **They are much** better now. **I think that** the whole neighbourhood loves them.
2 **I think we are going to go to** the beach this **afternoon**, but **I am a little** worried it might rain.
3 The concert was **really** good, the band **played well**, and the crowd was **very loud and excited**.

Answers

Answers start on page 120. You will also note that the answers are upside down. This is to hinder any easy copying of answers. After all they won't be available in the assessment, so it is important that you develop your own skills.
If you or your teacher would rather remove the answer pages, please cut along the dashed line to help preserve the binding.

Let's be accurate

The capital letter (page 48)

1 In November we are going to Sydney to see our old friend Barney.
2 Freddy and Fergus flew down to Wellington to go to Te Papa.
3 My brother Ashton hates hamburgers, but I love them.
4 I asked for a Lego set for my birthday because I love Lego.
5 We're going snowboarding in Taranaki on July 17th.

The full stop (.) (page 49)

1 This is a really easy chocolate cake recipe. It truly tastes of chocolate. It keeps for up to five days.
2 Venus is the second planet from the Sun. It is similar in size to Earth and it is the hottest planet in our solar system. Venus is named after the Roman goddess of love and beauty.
3 My room is extremely tidy. My sister's room is not. She has a desk with a volcano of books on top of it.
4 I love living in the city where there's so much to do every day. The shops and the cafes and the cinemas are always open. The city is a great place to live for someone like me.
5 I go to the skatepark every afternoon after school. It's the best place for me to practise for hours. If my mate Joe is around he comes too.

The question mark (?) (page 49)

1 'Will you come to the movie tomorrow?' asked Jill.
2 I'm going to the park. Do you want to come with me?
3 Our teacher always asks us if we're ready to start the lesson.
4 If it's sunny, why do I feel cold?
5 You're a Gemini, aren't you?

The exclamation mark (!) (page 50)

1 I am ready. Let's go right now!
2 Are we there yet? I can't wait to get there.
3 Will Joanie be there when we arrive?
4 We've been driving for hours and hours! Will we ever get there?
5 Look, there's the bach! We're here at last.

The comma (,) (pages 50–51)

1 My sister, who usually finishes all her dinner, suddenly refused to eat broccoli.
2 'I'm going to do my homework,' said Manu.
3 If you are afraid of the dark, take a torch with you.
4 Sally spoke in a whisper, 'Who's there? Show yourself.'
5 The sweetness of ice cream, often combined with flavours like chocolate, vanilla, caramel or fruits, provides a satisfying taste experience.

Speech marks ('...' or "...") (page 51)

1 The classroom was quiet as all the students focused on their writing.
'Sir, sir,' Thomas said suddenly, breaking the silence.
Mr Smith looked up from his book. 'What is it, Tom?' he asked.
'Look, there's a huge dog loose in the playground.'
'Where?' Mr Smith asked as he turned towards the windows. 'What kind of dog?'
2 My favourite book of all time has to be 'Under the Mountain'. It's set on Rangitoto Island and there's a book called 'Rangitoto' by Maria Gill that I've read too.
3 Titles like 'Finding Nemo', 'Toy Story', 'Moana' and 'Frozen' are often recommended for children to view. 'The Incredibles', 'Stuart Little' and 'Charlie and the Chocolate Factory' are also listed as good films for family movie nights.

The apostrophe (') (page 52)

1 Heng's favourite subject is biology because he's really interested in plants.
2 It might've been cool today but the sun's heat helped make the day warm.
3 It's hard to ride safely when my bike's lost its brakes.
4 Manu can't find his scooter because Tom's taken it to his house.
5 You cannot trust Smithy. He's a wolf in sheep's clothing.

Homophones (pages 53–54)

1 I'm building a table out of **wood**.
2 The protest was in support of **peace**.
3 You will **write** a letter to your koro **right** now.
4 When is it **your** birthday? If **you're** having a party, may I come?
5 Since last **week** I've been drinking **weak** tea.
6 The girl **knew** she needed a **new** pair of shoes.
7 The **stationary** car had lots of **stationery** in a box on the back seat.
8 I read a **tale** about a mermaid with a fish's **tail**.
9 The student wrote a **piece** about **peace** for the magazine.
10 The **weather** is sunny, but I can't decide **whether** to go outside or not.

Practice set 1 (page 55)

1 A
2 D
3 C
4 C
5 D
6 A
7 It's, dog's, children's
8 C

Practice set 2 (page 56)

1 A
2 B
3 B
4 D
5 C
6 D
7 C
8 good, well

Practice set 3 (page 57)

1 D
2 C
3 C
4 B
5 D
6 A
7 B
8 hear, whole

Practice set 4 (page 58)

1 D
2 D
3 C
4 C
5 B
6 said
7 D
8 C

Practice set 5 (page 59)

1 B
2 separated
3 D
4 A
5 B
6 D
7 C
8 D

Practice set 6 (page 60)

1 A
2 C
3 C
4 B
5 B
6 C
7 B
8 A

Practice set 7 (page 61)

1 A
2 B
3 C
4 B
5 D
6 brought, but
7 B
8 tomorrow

ISBN: 9780170499286

Answers

Let's get reading

HOW TO READ A TEXT

HAVE A GO ...

Pavlova Perfection (page 6)

1	C	**2**	B
3	C	**4**	A
5	D		

Start Smart, Hunt Better (page 8)

5	D	**6**	B
7	B	**8**	C

LET'S READ TOGETHER

Text 1: City Mission (pages 11–13)

1	C	**2**	B
3	C	**4**	C
5	A	**6**	C
7	D	**8**	C
9	D	**10**	C

Text 2: Niue (pages 14–15)

1	C	**2**	A
3	A	**4**	C
5	D	**6**	C

YOUR TURN

Text 3: Cicadas/Kihikihi/Tātarakihi (pages 16–17)

1	B	**2**	C
3	B	**4**	D
5	C	**6**	B
7	C	**8**	B

Text 4: Celebrating all things heroic (pages 18–19)

1	B	**2**	B
3	D	**4**	C
5	C	**6**	A
7	D	**8**	D

Text 5: Looking at droppings (pages 20–21)

1	A	**2**	C
3	B	**4**	B
5	D	**6**	C
7	C	**8**	D

Text 6: He Manu Taonga (pages 22–23)

1	C	**2**	A
3	A and D	**4**	B
5	C	**6**	D
7	B	**8**	D

Text 7: To Sign is to be Seen (pages 24–25)

1	C	**2**	C
3	C	**4**	B
5	D	**6**	C
7	A		

Text 8: Thinking Big – Pōtiki Poi (pages 26–27)

1	D	**2**	B
3	B	**4**	C
5	A	**6**	B
7	D	**8**	D

Text 9: Do BLUNT umbrellas flip inside out? (pages 28–29)

1	C	**2**	C
3	A	**4**	B
5	B	**6**	A
7	D	**8**	C
9	C		

Text 10: Beyond Circular Fashion (pages 30–33)

1	B	**2**	D
3	D	**4**	C
5	A	**6**	B
7	B	**8**	D
9	C	**10**	D
11	A	**12**	D

Text 11: Zebras of the fish world (pages 34–35)

1	C	**2**	B
3	D	**4**	A
5	D	**6**	B
7	C	**8**	D

Text 12: The story behind the popular New Zealand fashion label YOUKNOW (pages 36–37)

1	C	**2**	A
3	B	**4**	D
5	C	**6**	B
7	A		

Text 13: Discussing scam safety with your kids (pages 38–39)

1	D	**2**	B
3	C	**4**	D
5	A	**6**	C
7	D	**8**	C

Text 14 A and B: Tourism reviews (pages 40–41)

1	B	**2**	D
3	C	**4**	B
5	A	**6**	B
7	C	**8**	D
9	A		

Text 15 A and B: Diabetes pamphlet and Liam's story (pages 42–43)

1	C	**2**	B
3	D	**4**	B
5	C	**6**	A
7	D	**8**	C

Text 16 A and B: Far North author ... and Cuz (pages 44–46)

1	C	**2**	B
3	C	**4**	D
5	A	**6**	C
7	C	**8**	D
9	B		